# EARLY CHILDHOOD DIRECTOR'S MODEL LETTER KIT

## Over 240 Letters, Memos, Forms and More For Every Aspect of Your Job

Kathleen P. Watkins, Ed.D.
Lucius Durant, Jr., M. Ed.

The Center for Applied Research in Education
Paramus, New Jersey 07652

CIP Data is available from the Library of Congress

Watkins, Kathleen Pullan.
    Early childhood director's model letter kit / Kathleen Pullan Watkins & Lucius Durant, Jr.
      p.  cm.
    ISBN 0-13-092649-3
     1. Early childhood education—Administration—Forms.   2. Schools—Records and
correspondence—Forms.   3. Form letters.   I. Durant, Lucius. 1932.   II. Title.

LB2822.6 .W38   2002
651.7'52—dc21

2002019801

Printed in the United States of America

*10 9 8 7 6 5 4 3 2 1*

ISBN 0-13-092649-3

**THE CENTER FOR APPLIED RESEARCH
IN EDUCATION**
**Paramus, New Jersey 07652**

http://www.phdirect.com

Dedicated with love to
our grandchildren
and
all little ones in
child care and preschool

# About the Authors

**Kathleen Pullan Watkins,** Ed.D., received her education at Antioch and Temple Universities. She has worked as a teacher in and director of many child-care programs, and as a teacher trainer for more than twenty years. Presently Dr. Watkins is Associate Professor of Early Childhood Education at Community College of Philadelphia where she instructs and supervises student teachers planning careers with young children. She coordinates the T.E.A.C.H. Program at the College that provides scholarships for employed child-care workers. Dr. Watkins is the co-author of seven other early childhood resources, including *The Complete Book of Forms for Managing the Early Childhood Program*. She is the mother of Matthew and Alyson and grandmother of Sydney Indigo.

**Lucius Durant, Jr.,** M.Ed., is an educator with a lifelong passion for learning and teaching. He has served in a full range of teaching and administrative positions in the early childhood education field. As a partner in Durant and Watkins Associates, Mr. Durant has co-authored five books. In retirement, he continues to be an active partner in Durant and Watkins Associates while enjoying his grandchildren and volunteering in community activities.

# ABOUT THIS KIT

Studies supporting the significance of the first five years of life have led to a proliferation of child-care, preschool, family child-care, and nursery school programs in the last decade. According to current data, there are more than 235,000 licensed child-care centers and family child-care homes[1], and 18,200 Head Start Centers[2] in the United States.

There have also been some long-awaited developments in the early childhood profession. Funds have increased for programming and for the training of teachers. The business community has taken an interest in the education of preschoolers, and in some states has thrown considerable support behind legislative and funding initiatives. Centers and family child-care homes have begun the self-study process leading to accreditation by the National Association for the Education of Young Children, raising the quality bar for early childhood programs nationally.

These efforts have been many and varied around the country, but all are leading in one consistent direction. That is, a recognition within the field and the nation-at-large of the significance of the work of the early childhood profession. As we move with finality away from the belief that our work is mere "baby sitting," there comes the responsibility for increased accountability. Accountability refers to the ways that we conduct business, keep records, evaluate our programs, and communicate with others. The assumption of accountability extends beyond the role of the program administrator. All of those who are involved in early childhood programs—teachers, support staff, board members, and volunteers—must all share the responsibility for program outcomes.

As the demand for accountability increases, directors and other program leaders are not automatically equipped to respond. Some programs are administered by leaders with academic credentials in early childhood education; others by individuals with related backgrounds in education or psychology; and a third group of programs have business persons functioning as directors. What is common to virtually all of these situations is that there is little formal training for early childhood education leadership. Even when formerly schooled in the care and education of children, teachers seldom receive the background necessary to take the helm of a comprehensive children's program. Across the country, unless one is fortunate to be mentored by another administrator, much of the training for leadership occurs on-the-job.

This book is designed to support all of those directing programs for young children. We accomplish this by providing a quick and time-saving resource for the busy administrator who works with a wide range of persons, and by suggesting some forms of interaction with center clients and others to enhance the overall program. In other words, we hope that the topics of some of these letters will suggest to directors additional program components and constituents, such as new relationships with local businesses or additional opportunities for family involvement.

---

[1]National Child Care Information Center, 2000
[2]Head Start Bureau, 2001

We want readers to notice the tone and style of these written communications with parents, children, and staff. These connote respect and send a clear message about the administrator's desire to include them as a part of the center family. The tone of these letters is designed to develop and increase the opportunities for additional interaction.

Many letters are also designed to be informative. Not only do they suggest a style of communicating for business purposes, but they also introduce some administrators to sources of service and ideas.

This book is divided into five segments: communications with parents (Section 1), children (Section 2), teachers and staff (Section 3), board and community members (Section 4), and consultants and contractors (Section 5). Headings found in the Contents indicate the subject of each letter. Letters have blank spaces provided so that information pertinent to each program may be inserted. Letters can be utilized in traditional forms, can be modified to suit individual program needs, or can be employed as e-mail messages where appropriate. We have also included some additional kinds of communiqués, such as a year-end report, a newsletter, a staff evaluation, and child progress reports. These, too, are important ways of interacting with the early childhood community. Lastly, many letters include art designed to enhance their professional appearance.

Throughout the book readers will note mention of various manuals appropriate for use in early childhood education programs; these include *Parents, Staff,* and *Volunteer Handbooks*. These manuals should be developed by administrators and be reflective of the programs they represent. Handbooks like these play an important role in conveying program policies and procedures to families, staff, and the community.

However edifying, the contents of this book should not be considered all inclusive. Each administrator must review the components of his or her own program to assure that all involved parties receive the information necessary to support active participation. Further, assignment of a letter or other communication to a section does not indicate its exclusivity to a population. Newsletters and year-end reports, for example, should be shared with all who are involved with or interested in the program. Regular communications are a vital record of individual and program activities, and yield the rewards of enhanced relationships.

We salute all of those who have shouldered the challenge of guiding programs for our youngest and most vulnerable children.

*Kathleen Pullan Watkins*
*Lucius Durant, Jr.*

# CONTENTS

# SECTION TWO
## LETTERS AND CERTIFICATES FOR CHILDREN

# SECTION THREE
## LETTERS TO TEACHERS AND STAFF

## SECTION FOUR
### LETTERS TO BOARD AND COMMUNITY MEMBERS

## SECTION FIVE
### LETTERS TO CONSULTANTS AND CONTRACTORS

# LETTERS TO PARENTS AND OTHER PRIMARY CARETAKERS

Regular and effective communication with parents of children who receive services from a school or program is as critical an activity as any a director will engage in. It is not enough to have a parent-involvement component via a few teachers or other staff. A program administrator sets the tone and creates an atmosphere in which relationships with parents either flourish or stagnate. One of the roles of the director is to assure that parents receive recurring feedback on the progress of their children. Families must also be kept appraised of the policies of the program, and the types of activities that their children are engaging in. Additionally, young children have a strong and symbiotic tie to their parents. In a literal sense, to ignore the significance of family in the lives of preschool-aged children is to disregard an important part of the children themselves.

An early childhood leader must welcome families into the program; assist in creating the policies that impact on families and staff; respond to the issues that arise when procedures are not observed; assist parents as they cope with problems impacting on them and their children; and resolve home–school conflicts. Direction of a early childhood program is a multifaceted job, and among the greatest of responsibilities is supporting parenting competence and overall family needs. Correspondence with parents and other primary caretakers must be undertaken with tact and courtesy. Underlying all interactions with parents must be the knowledge that the feelings we engender in the adults impact heavily on children's levels of comfort and success in the program.

Correspondence with parents will be of a positive, supportive nature; some serves as a reminder about policies. When written communications with families address a wide range of topics, parents are reassured that they are being treated with equity and respect. If correspondence is reserved only for infraction of rules, then relationships with administrators assume a punitive tone. A letter from their child's early childhood program becomes equivalent to a summons to the principal's office.

Directors must also keep in mind the power of their correspondence to help or hinder parents' individual growth. This Section also contains several certificates that can be presented for services rendered or as a means to increase parents' self-esteem.

It is within the scope of a director's responsibility to convey many types of information to families, but when that role can be taken in a compassionate and supportive fashion, home–school ties can be maintained and strengthened.

1

# WELCOME BACK TO SCHOOL

Dear Children and Parents:

Welcome back to the Center. We hope that you have had a restful and enjoyable holiday!

Just a reminder that young children are less attuned to the passage of time than we adults are. To them an absence of a few days, weeks, or months may seem like a long time. Children often need a few days to readjust once they have returned to school. If your child seems unusually upset at the idea of returning to the Center or at drop off in the morning, please bring it to the attention of the

teachers so that we can provide support. You can help your child look forward to the day's activities by reminding him or her of special friends or equipment that he or she enjoys. Let your child know that friends at school look forward to seeing him or her each day. Once your child has returned to the weekly routine, any distress should disappear.

We want to thank those parents/guardians who have completed the contract for services for this year. If you have not done so, we need to receive the contract no later than _____. A copy is enclosed with this letter.

Together we can help your child enjoy and benefit from the Center Program.

Sincerely,

_____
Center Director

FIGURE 1.1

# PARENT–CENTER CONTRACT FOR SERVICES

I, _____, parent/guardian of
(parent's name)

_____, hereby contract for school/
(child's name)

child care/after-school services with _____.
(agency name)

I have read the *Parents' Handbook* and am aware of and agree to all the guidelines and my responsibilities surrounding my child's enrollment in this Program.

The type of services contracted for is _____.

The hours of service are _____.

The date of start of services is _____.

The fee for services is _____ per _____.

_____     _____
Parent's/Guardian's Signature                    Date

_____     _____
Center Representative                                   Date

# INTRODUCTION TO *PARENTS' HANDBOOK*

Dear Parents:

We are pleased to count you and your child as part of our Center family. Our primary goal is to offer your child a safe and healthy environment designed to promote development. We are here to support you in the joyous yet serious task of raising your child, and hope to be your partners in this effort. Please feel free to question us daily about your child's activities and moods. Sharing your child's home life will similarly better equip us to help him or her.

The *Parents' Handbook* is provided to families so that we each will know what to expect of the other. A review of the contents for the *Handbook* reveals that it contains information on the program philosophy, goals and objectives, an overview of the curriculum for children, and statements of center policy and procedures. It is our hope that you will take time to read the *Handbook* carefully, and will question us regarding any unclear points.

Working together we can set your child on the road to a healthy and happy childhood full of wonder and the joy of learning.

Please contact the Center at _____ at any time with your questions. Thank you for your cooperation and support of the Program.

Sincerely,


_____
Center Director

# WELCOME TO A NEW FAMILY

## Child Care Center

Dear _____ Family:

Along with the staff, I would like to take this opportunity to welcome you to our early childhood program. We know that you and _____ will spend many happy hours of play and learning at the Center.

During your initial interview, you received a copy of our *Parents' Handbook*. Please take time to review all of the Center's policies and procedures, then sign and return the attached slip to me. I am available to answer any questions that you might have.

We are aware that raising children can be both stressful and complicated, and hope that you will consider us your partners in this effort. If situations arise that affect your child's health or emotional well-being, please advise us.

Thank you for choosing our program for your child's care and education.

Sincerely,


_____
Center Director

- - - - - - - - - - - - - - - - - - - - - - - - - - - - - - - - - -

Dear Center Director:

I have read and understand the policies of the program, and agree to observe the guidelines described in the *Parents' Handbook*.

Parent/Guardian Signature _____ Date _____

# FIRST-WEEK-OF-SCHOOL SCHEDULE

## Child Care Center

Dear _____ Family:

    We are delighted to welcome you and your child, _____, to our program! Just a reminder about our policies regarding the first week of school that are outlined in the *Parents' Handbook*.

    Since young children need time and support in order to adjust to a new setting, we require that you or another primary caretaker stay with your child during the first two days of attendance. On the first day, you and your child will stay for two hours only, and, on the second day, you and your child will come for the morning and leave after lunch. On the third day, your child may stay on his or her own at the Center, but must be picked up immediately after lunch and before the children take their naps. On the fourth day of attendance, your child may stay at the Center for the entire day.

    We are aware that this requirement can create a hardship for parents employed outside the home, or those with extensive family commitments. However, we know that this investment of your time will reap the rewards of a happy and well-adjusted child.

    Thank you for your cooperation in this matter.

Sincerely,


_____

Center Director

# SUPPLIES FOR SCHOOL

Dear Parents:

Your child will need the following supplies for the start of the school year. Although the Center supplies most things needed by children, your child must have the items below. Please label all items with your child's name.

- change of clothing (pants, shirt, underclothes, socks)
- plastic paint smock (covering chest and legs)
- small blanket for naptime
- child-sized toothbrush
- a lunch box with Thermos

Thank you for your cooperation and support of the Program.

Sincerely,

_____

Center Director

© 2002 by The Center for Applied Research in Education

# BUS SERVICE

Dear Parents:

Transportation by Center bus or van will begin on _____. Your child's pickup time is _____. Bus/van drivers are instructed to wait no longer than two minutes for a child, so please have your child ready at the scheduled time. Children must be escorted to the bus or van by an adult. Drivers cannot come to the door to retrieve your child.

Once on the bus or van, your child must take a seat and remain in that seat until arrival at the Center. Aides will ride on each bus or van to supervise children. If a child is unable to remain seated during the ride to the Center, transportation privileges may be forfeited. Please contact the Center at _____ with any questions regarding transportation.

Thank you for your cooperation and support of the Program.

Sincerely,

_____

Center Director

# HEALTH INFORMATION RECORDS

Dear Parents:

The Center is required to keep up-to-date records of children's immunizations and dental care. At this time our records indicate that we are missing _____ information for your child. We cannot continue to provide services for your child if records are not updated by _____. We trust that you will forward the missing records to us as soon as possible. Please contact the Center at _____ with any questions regarding your child's health records.

Thank you for your cooperation and support of the program.

Sincerely,

_____

Center Director

# PARENT VOLUNTEER QUESTIONNAIRE

Dear _____:

    Once again, welcome to you and your child. The next few weeks will be filled with a variety of new experiences and challenges, and we hope to support you in whatever ways are required. As you know from meeting with various staff, we believe that a strong parent involvement component is key to the success of the overall program, as well as that of the individual child. Parent involvement helps parents to know and participate in implementing the curriculum; to get to know staff and other families; and to keep abreast of children's unique developmental changes. Please take a few minutes to complete the questionnaire below, and return it to the Center when you next drop off your child. This information will provide us with tools to best use the talents and time that you can contribute to our Program. Thank you in advance for your cooperation.

Sincerely,

_____

Center Director

------------------------------------------------

**Parent Volunteer Questionnaire**

I am available to volunteer at the Center on _____ from _____
                                                  (day)

until _____.

    I am unable to volunteer hours at the Center, but I am able to:

    ____ Participate in a telephone tree.
    ____ Collect materials for use in children's curriculum projects.
    ____ Help to publish a newsletter.
    ____ Identify speakers/topics for monthly parents' meetings.
    ____ Plan special events for the Center.
    ____ Participate in fundraising for the Center.
    ____ other _____

Special talents/interests include _____. The best time to reach me is _____.

Parent's/Guardian's Signature _____ Date _____

# SUPPORTING THE CURRICULUM

Dear Parents:

As you know from reading the *Parents' Handbook*, the Center offers a developmentally-appropriate curriculum that is designed to enhance the overall growth of your child. However, we cannot be successful without your assistance. This is not the assistance that comes from volunteer hours, although these are crucial to us, too. Rather, this support comes from your interactions with your child, the questions that you ask about the day, the comments that you make in response to your child's description of the program, and the activities that you engage in at home with your child. You will also be asked from time to time to conduct specific follow-up activities, as a way of reinforcing the learning at the Center. *This is not homework.* Homework is assigned once a child reaches elementary school. These are meant to be enjoyable parent and child times that support your child's school learning.

What follows are some tips for supporting the Center curriculum on an everyday basis. Please contact us with your questions about these ideas or anything your child may be learning at school.

### Guidelines for Supporting Your Child's Everyday Learning

1. Check the Center bulletin boards daily for a review of the day's activities.
2. Ask the teacher about any unfamiliar activities.
3. Start the day by reminding your child about something he or she will be doing at school, for example: "You will see your friend Jonathan" or "Today is the trip to the Zoo."
4. Each day, ask your child, "How was school today? What did you do?" If your child says, "Nothing" or "We ate cookies" (they often do), probe a bit. Ask, "What kind of cookies did you eat?" or "Did you go outside today?"
5. Read to your child daily, at least one age-appropriate book. For help with selecting books, talk to your child's teacher. It is helpful when you can read a book that addresses something that your child is learning about at the Center.
6. Ask your child about his or her friends and teachers at school. If your child tells you that he or she especially likes or dislikes someone, ask why. This can give insights as to how your child feels about the school experience.

© 2002 by The Center for Applied Research in Education

# APPROPRIATE CLOTHING FOR SCHOOL

Dear Parents:

A reminder that, as stated in the *Parents' Handbook*, children should be dressed in weather-appropriate play clothes for attendance at the Center. Expensive clothes will only be damaged by the play and activities of the child's school day. The Center cannot be responsible for tears or stains to clothing that occur in the course of normal play.

When your child dresses in play clothes, he or she feels free to participate in all activities without restriction. On any given day, your child might play with paints, clay, sand, or water; go to the playground; or make a vegetable or fruit salad. These and other activities are designed to enhance your child's intellectual, motor, and social skills. We do not worry (nor should your child) about a bit of paint or dirt stain on clothing. It simply means that your child has had fun and interesting learning experiences.

Please help ensure a good day by dressing your child for play!

Sincerely,

_____

Center Director

# CHANGE OF CLOTHING

Dear Parents:

Young children have toileting accidents, food spills, and generally get messy. That is why the Center requires the children to have a fresh change of clothing in their cubbies, including pants, shirt, underclothes, and socks.

It is difficult for your child if an accident occurs and there are no clean clothes. Please bring a fresh change of clothing each time soiled clothes are sent home.

Thank you for your cooperation!

Sincerely,

_____

Center Director

# LUNCHES AND SNACKS BROUGHT FROM HOME

Dear Parents:

We like to occasionally remind parents about the importance of nutritious meals for young children. Although packing meals at home for school is time consuming, the types of foods that your child finds in his or her lunch box help to determine the energy that he or she has for participating in school activities. When selecting foods for snacks or lunches from home for your child, please consider those that are low in fat, sodium, and sugar. For example, some of the ready-made snacks or luncheon meals are high on kid eye-appeal, but low on nutritional value. Also low in nutrition are the canned pasta meals. Please note that fast-food meals of any kind are not permitted at the Center.

When choosing cookies or other snack foods, please read the labels. While an occasional cookie, sweet, or chip is all right, we discourage parents from sending these foods to school daily.

It may take a few extra minutes, but it is worth your time to make a peanut butter or cheese sandwich and add a piece of fruit for your child's lunch. Yogurt, fruit roll-ups, and fresh fruit make nutritious snacks. Always advise the teachers of foods that require refrigeration. Please help us educate your child about nutritious eating and snacking so that he or she will benefit from these lessons now and in the future!

Sincerely,

_____

Center Director

# CHILD DROP-OFF/PICKUP SAFETY

Dear Parents:

Please remember that Center policies (see *Parents' Handbook*) require that parents deliver children to the classroom door and sign in when dropping them off at the Center. Children may not be left in the Center yard or inside the door of the classroom. Teachers should be made aware that each child has arrived for the day.

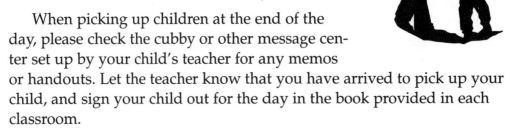

When picking up children at the end of the day, please check the cubby or other message center set up by your child's teacher for any memos or handouts. Let the teacher know that you have arrived to pick up your child, and sign your child out for the day in the book provided in each classroom.

Children should be dropped off and picked up from the Center only by designated persons 18 years of age or older. Children will not be released to minors. If a substitute caregiver is designated by you to transport your child to and from school, please notify the Center at _____ of the name of this individual and the times/days that he/she will be providing this service.

These policies are designed to provide the utmost safety for your child. Thank you for your cooperation.

Sincerely,


_____
Center Director

# MEDICATIONS POLICY

Dear Parents:

Center policies, as described in the *Parents' Handbook* and state guidelines for programs like ours, state that we can only administer medications to children if a strict set of guidelines is observed.

These guidelines are as follows:

- Medications must come in their original bottles.
- The name of the child to whom medications are to be administered must be on the bottle. Medications cannot be shared by siblings.
- The medication dosage must be on the bottle, including the number of times per day to be administered and instructions as to how long the medication should be administered.
- Let us know which food products (e.g., dairy) should be avoided while your child is taking medication.
- Teachers will store medications in a lock box and/or in the refrigerator according to storage instructions.
- The same teacher will administer medications each day to avoid confusion.
- Teachers will record each dosage of medications given in a book for this purpose found in each classroom.

Please assist us in the proper administration of medications to your child.

Sincerely,

_____

Center Director

# PERMISSION FOR SPECIAL SERVICES

## Child Care Center

Dear _____:

As per our discussion on _____, we would like to refer your child for _____ services. These services would be provided by _____ at the child care center, and the cost to you would be _____. All information about these services and the results of tests or therapies is confidential, and would be shared with staff only as needed to plan for your child.

Please sign below to indicate your permission for your child to receive these services, and return this permission form to your child's teacher as soon as possible.

Sincerely,

_____
Center Director

- - - - - - - - - - - - - - - - - - - - - - -

### Permission for Special Services

____ I do give my permission for my child to receive _____ services at the Center. I understand that these services are to be provided by _____ and that the cost for services is _____.

____ I do not give permission for my child to receive _____ services at the Center.

Parent(s)/Guardian Signature _____ Date _____

# CENTER NEWSLETTER

Dear Parents:

Each month we publish a newsletter, *Voice from the Center*, for our families, Board, and community members. It is designed to provide an update on events and activities at the Center, and to familiarize all with our staff and services. We welcome your input and ideas for articles. Some suggestions include family birthdays, births and other special events, favorite recipes, health and safety tips, and services offered by parents and staff.

The deadline for each month's newsletter is the 15th. Story or article ideas submitted after that date may be held for the next month. All suggestions must be submitted on the forms provided in the Center office, signed by the submitter, and dated.

If you have an idea for the next newsletter, please use the tear-off portion of this letter and drop it off in the main office by the 15th. Each idea used in the newsletter will be credited to the individual suggesting it.

We look forward to your ideas!

Sincerely,

_____
Center Director

- - - - - - - - - - - - - - - - - - - - - - - - - - - - - - - - -

**Newsletter Suggestions**

My idea for a newsletter article is (for recipes, please attach a complete recipe):

_____

_____

_____

_____

_____

_____

Submitted by _____ Date _____

# CENTER VISITORS/OBSERVATIONS

**Child Care Center**

Dear Parents:

Parents and other immediate family members are always welcome to volunteer, visit, or to observe in the classroom. No prior notice is necessary. However, if you are planning to stay with us for the morning, please advise the classroom teacher that you will be staying and the capacity in which you will be participating.

Non-family members or other visitors to the Center must provide 24-hour notice of the observation and the reason for the visit. Non-family members not approved by the Center staff as volunteers will not ordinarily be permitted to work with the children.

Observation of these policies helps to assure the safety and comfort of staff and children.

Sincerely,

_____

Center Director

# PERMISSION FOR PHOTOGRAPHS/VIDEOTAPING

Dear Parents:

Occasionally the Center staff or approved visitors take pictures of or videotape the children. These pictures (still or moving) are used to publicize and promote Center activities or events. Pictures may appear in local newspapers, center brochures, or on television. No additional notice may be given of picture-taking sessions.

A form is attached for parental approval/release for photographs. Please sign and date the attached form and return it immediately to the Center. No photos or video will be taken of children whose parents do not grant permission.

Sincerely,

_____
Center Director

- - - - - - - - - - - - - - - - - - - - - - - - - - - - - - - -

**Permission for Photographs/Videotape**

_____ I do give permission for my child to be photographed or videotaped while at the Center or on Center-sponsored field trips for purposes of promoting the Center and its activities.

_____ I do not give permission for my child to be photographed or videotaped while at the Center or on Center-sponsored field trips for purposes of promoting the Center and its activities.

Parent(s)/Guardian Signature _____ Date _____

# NOTICE OF TESTING

Dear Parents:

During the week of _____, teachers will be administering standardized developmental tests to children in the Program. These tests are designed only to assure that children are meeting developmental norms for their age group. These are not intelligence or aptitude tests. These are not paper-and-pencil tests. Children will be observed during activities that are similar to those that they are involved in every day.

To enable your child to do his or her best when tested, we recommend that you make sure that your child has a good night's sleep and a nutritious breakfast. We also recommend that your child be dressed comfortably so that teachers can best assess physical motor skills.

At the end of testing, the results will be analyzed by computer by an independent company, and the results will be returned to the Center. During test analysis, children will be identified only by a code number. When results of the tests are available, families will be notified and conferences will be scheduled for those parents who wish to discuss them with their children's teachers. We expect results to be available during the week of _____ and will notify you at that time.

Thank you for your cooperation in this matter.

Sincerely,

_____
Center Director

# RESULTS OF STANDARDIZED TESTS

Dear Parents:

Results of the standardized child developmental tests conducted at the Center are now available. Teachers are available to meet with parents during the week of _____ to discuss the results with you. Please contact the Center at _____ if you wish to schedule an appointment.

Sincerely,

_____

Center Director

# PARENT–TEACHER CONFERENCES

Dear Parents:

Parent–teacher conferences are held three times each year at the Center to keep parents informed of children's progress. This is an opportunity for a one-on-one interaction with your child's teacher. Conferences are one-half hour long, and child care is available during the conferences. We do not encourage parents to bring their children into the conferences.

Upcoming conferences will be held during the weeks of _____ and _____. Each classroom teacher has a variety of days and times available for conferences. You will find the conference schedule for your child's teacher posted in the classroom. Early sign-ups assure that parents get the days and times most convenient for them.

If there are questions about conferences that the director can answer, please contact me at _____. We look forward to seeing you at conference time.

Sincerely,

_____

Center Director

# HOME VISITS

## Child Care Center

Dear Parents:

During the week of ＿＿＿＿＿＿, teachers will be available to make visits to children's homes. Home visits are entirely optional, but they do provide an opportunity for teachers to see children outside the Center environment. Children are often excited and pleased to have their teachers as guests in their homes.

Home visits generally last one-half hour and can usually be scheduled at times mutually convenient to parents and teachers. Your child's teacher will contact you in the next few days to ask whether you are interested in a home visit.

Thank you in advance for welcoming us into your home.

Sincerely,

＿＿＿＿＿＿＿＿＿＿＿＿＿＿＿＿

Center Director

# SCHOOL PICTURE DAY

Dear Parents:

That best of all days has arrived! On _____ from _____ until _____, a photographer from the _____ School Picture Company will be at the Center to take your child's photograph. This is the one day when dressing up your child is encouraged. There is no fee for the initial pictures. When proofs are available, you will receive these along with a price list for picture packages. These packages are expected to range in price from _____ to _____. Please note that all proofs must be returned to the Picture Company.

A class photo will also be taken with the teachers from each class-room. These will be available for separate purchase from your child's individual photos.

If you have questions regarding picture day, please contact the Center at _____.

Sincerely,

_____

Center Director

# CHILD PROGRESS REPORTS

Child Care Center

Dear Parents:

During the next few weeks, teachers will be completing Child Progress Reports. Sample reports are provided in the *Parents' Handbook*. Reports provide parents with information about the developmental skills their children have acquired, as well as those still evolving. Strategies for assisting children at home with skills development will also be provided. These reports will be ready for your review at the next parent–teacher conferences coming up in _____.

We will be pleased to answer your questions about your child's report at that time.

Sincerely,

_____

Center Director

FIGURE 1.2

# CHILD PROGRESS REPORT:
# PRESCHOOL LEVEL

# Child Care Center

Dear Parent(s):

Enclosed you will find the semiannual Child Progress Report describing your child's development and progress while attending the Child Care Center. You will find that there are sections covering the physical, cognitive (intellectual), language, social, emotional, and self-help skills of your child.

If the Child Progress Report indicates with a check mark that your child "Has Mastered" a skill, then this skill is well-developed in your child. A check in the column labeled "Beginning to Master" means that your child is working on this skill. Your child may simply be too young to have fully developed this ability, but will soon have this skill.

At the bottom of each page are spaces for "Comments" and "Home Strategies." The "Comments" space is where the teacher will put written remarks about your child's progress in this skill area. The section for "Home Strategies" is where the teacher will make suggestions for ways that you can work at home with your child to develop these skills.

On the last page of the Child Progress Report, the teacher will complete the section called "School Strategies." This page tells you what the teacher is planning to do to assist your child in school in the upcoming months.

We hope that you will find the Child Progress Report helpful. Please let the teachers know if you have comments about this report.

Thank you for your interest in and support of our program.

Sincerely,


_____          _____
Center Director                                  Teacher

# CHILD PROGRESS REPORT:
## PRESCHOOL LEVEL

CHILD'S NAME _____ TEACHER _____

DATE OF BIRTH _____ REPORT DATE _____

| | Has Mastered | Beginning to Master |
|---|---|---|
| **I. PHYSICAL DEVELOPMENT** **Gross Motor Skills** | | |
| A. Has age-appropriate balance and coordination | _____ | _____ |
| B. Walks, runs, and climbs stairs with ease | _____ | _____ |
| C. Moves body to music | _____ | _____ |
| D. Turns simple somersault | _____ | _____ |
| E. Stacks and builds with blocks | _____ | _____ |
| F. Imitates hopping and jumping upon request | _____ | _____ |
| **Fine Motor Skills** | | |
| G. Uses scissors, crayons, and paint brushes | _____ | _____ |
| H. Puts together 5- to 12-piece puzzles | _____ | _____ |
| I. Uses peg boards and stacking toys easily | _____ | _____ |
| J. Pours liquid from a small pitcher with little spillage | _____ | _____ |
| K. Copies simple shapes | _____ | _____ |

COMMENTS: _____

_____

_____


HOME STRATEGIES: _____

_____

_____

# CHILD PROGRESS REPORT
## (continued)

CHILD'S NAME _____ Date _____

|  | Has Mastered | Beginning to Master |
|---|---|---|
| **II. COGNITIVE DEVELOPMENT** | | |
| A. Gives own name upon request | _____ | _____ |
| B. Names basic shapes (square, circle, triangle) | _____ | _____ |
| C. Names primary colors (red, blue, yellow) | _____ | _____ |
| D. Identifies basic similarities and differences in objects | _____ | _____ |
| E. Puts objects into sets (e.g., things with wheels) | _____ | _____ |
| F. Matches identical objects or pictures | _____ | _____ |
| G. Matches items that belong together (e.g., knife/fork) | _____ | _____ |
| H. Counts aloud from one to ten | _____ | _____ |
| I. Solves simple word problems (e.g., "What will happen if you wear your bathing suit in the snow?") | _____ | _____ |
| J. Sees simple patterns in objects (e.g., leaves that are the same shape) | _____ | _____ |
| K. Repeats simple patterns (e.g., pattern of red, blue, and green beads) | _____ | _____ |
| L. Relates events in sequence | _____ | _____ |
| M. Has age-appropriate attention span | _____ | _____ |
| N. Sets table with one cup, napkin, plate, spoon per place | _____ | _____ |

COMMENTS _____

_____

_____

HOME STRATEGIES _____

_____

_____

# CHILD PROGRESS REPORT
## (continued)

CHILD'S NAME _____ Date _____

|  | Has Mastered | Beginning to Master |
|---|---|---|
| **III. LANGUAGE DEVELOPMENT** | | |
| A. Has age-appropriate vocabulary | _____ | _____ |
| B. Uses comparative terms (e.g., big/little, tall/short) | _____ | _____ |
| C. Participates in conversation as both speaker and listener | _____ | _____ |
| D. Follows a short sequence of verbal directions | _____ | _____ |
| E. Listens attentively and recounts events from stories | _____ | _____ |
| F. Names body parts | _____ | _____ |
| G. Responds to questions with appropriate answers | _____ | _____ |
| H. Describes persons or events shown in photographs | _____ | _____ |
| I. Looks at books | _____ | _____ |
| J. Recognizes and names some letters | _____ | _____ |
| K. Has age-appropriate articulation | _____ | _____ |
| L. Constructs and uses simple sentences | _____ | _____ |

COMMENTS _____

_____

_____

_____

HOME STRATEGIES _____

_____

_____

_____

# CHILD PROGRESS REPORT
## (continued)

CHILD'S NAME _____ Date _____

|  | | Has Mastered | Beginning to Master |
|---|---|---|---|
| **IV.** | **SOCIAL SKILLS** | | |
| A. | Can play alone at times | _____ | _____ |
| B. | Enjoys play with one or more other children | _____ | _____ |
| C. | Can wait briefly for own turn | _____ | _____ |
| D. | Occasionally shares toys or materials with others | _____ | _____ |
| E. | Enjoys conversation with adults and children | _____ | _____ |
| F. | Usually follows established rules | _____ | _____ |
| G. | Respects the property of other children | _____ | _____ |
| H. | Can lead a group | _____ | _____ |
| I. | Can follow another child who is group leader | _____ | _____ |
| J. | Enjoys playing a variety of roles in fantasy play (e.g., mother, baby, firefighter, superhero, etc.) | _____ | _____ |
| K. | Enjoys winning games | _____ | _____ |
| L. | Applauds others who win | _____ | _____ |
| M. | Enjoys helping adults | _____ | _____ |

COMMENTS _____

_____

_____

_____

HOME STRATEGIES _____

_____

_____

_____

# CHILD PROGRESS REPORT
## (continued)

CHILD'S NAME _____ Date _____

|  | | Has Mastered | Beginning to Master |
|---|---|---|---|
| **V.** | **EMOTIONAL DEVELOPMENT** | | |
| | A. Separates easily from parent(s) | _____ | _____ |
| | B. Expresses a broad range of emotions | _____ | _____ |
| | C. Tries to describe feelings verbally | _____ | _____ |
| | D. Shows attachment to other children and adults | _____ | _____ |
| | E. Expresses affection for others | _____ | _____ |
| | F. Expresses hostility or anger toward others | _____ | _____ |
| | G. Shares adult attention with other children | _____ | _____ |
| | H. Clearly expresses needs, likes, and dislikes | _____ | _____ |
| | I. Shows ownership of toys and materials | _____ | _____ |
| | J. Shows pride in possessions and accomplishments | _____ | _____ |

COMMENTS _____

_____

_____

_____

HOME STRATEGIES _____

_____

_____

_____

# CHILD PROGRESS REPORT
## (continued)

CHILD'S NAME _____ Date _____

|  | | Has Mastered | Beginning to Master |
|---|---|---|---|
| **VI. SELF-HELP SKILLS** | | | |
| A. | Dresses self in coat, socks, shoes | _____ | _____ |
| B. | Washes and dries own hands | _____ | _____ |
| C. | Brushes teeth | _____ | _____ |
| D. | Uses fork and spoon | _____ | _____ |
| E. | Serves self at mealtimes | _____ | _____ |
| F. | Sets and clears own place at table | _____ | _____ |
| G. | Wipes mouth with napkin after meals | _____ | _____ |
| H. | Toilets self unassisted | _____ | _____ |
| I. | Fastens clothing after toileting | _____ | _____ |
| J. | Asks for adult assistance as needed | _____ | _____ |

COMMENTS _____

_____

_____

HOME STRATEGIES _____

_____

_____

SCHOOL STRATEGIES _____

_____

_____

_____

_____

FIGURE 1.3

# CHILD PROGRESS REPORT:
## TODDLER LEVEL

# Child Care Center

Dear Parent(s):

Enclosed you will find the semiannual Child Progress Report describing your child's development and progress while attending the Child Care Center. You will find that there are sections covering the physical, cognitive (intellectual), language, social, emotional, and self-help skills of your child.

If the Child Progress Report indicates with a check mark that your child "Has Mastered" a skill, then this skill is well-developed in your child. A check in the column labeled "Beginning to Master" means that your child is working on this skill. Your child may simply be too young to have fully developed this ability, but will soon have this skill.

At the bottom of each page are spaces for "Comments" and "Home Strategies." The "Comments" space is where the teacher will put written remarks about your child's progress in this skill area. The section for "Home Strategies" is where the teacher will make suggestions for ways that you can work at home with your child to develop these skills.

On the last page of the Child Progress Report, the teacher will complete the section called "School Strategies." This page tells you what the teacher is planning to do to assist your child in school in the upcoming months.

We hope that you will find the Child Progress Report helpful. Please let the teachers know if you have comments about this report.

Thank you for your interest in and support of our program.

Sincerely,

_____          _____
Center Director                                      Teacher

# CHILD PROGRESS REPORT: TODDLER LEVEL

CHILD'S NAME _____ TEACHER _____

DATE OF BIRTH _____ REPORT DATE _____

| | Has Mastered | Beginning to Master |
|---|---|---|
| **I. PHYSICAL DEVELOPMENT** | | |
| **Gross Motor Skills** | | |
| A. Has age-appropriate balance and coordination | _____ | _____ |
| B. Walks alone | _____ | _____ |
| C. Climbs steps with assistance (adult or stair railing) | _____ | _____ |
| D. Imitates adult body movements with reasonable similarity | _____ | _____ |
| E. Pushes and pulls toys (e.g., wagons and toy cars) | _____ | _____ |
| F. Climbs over small obstacles | _____ | _____ |
| G. Runs awkwardly | _____ | _____ |
| H. Pushes self along on wheeled toy | _____ | _____ |
| I. Kicks a large ball forward for a short distance | _____ | _____ |
| J. Throws a small ball forward for a short distance | _____ | _____ |
| **Fine Motor Skills** | | |
| K. Holds spoon, crayon, and large paint brush | _____ | _____ |
| L. Manipulates clay and fingerpaint | _____ | _____ |
| M. Puts together puzzles of three to five pieces | _____ | _____ |

COMMENTS _____

_____

_____

HOME STRATEGIES _____

_____

_____

# CHILD PROGRESS REPORT
## (continued)

CHILD'S NAME _____ Date _____

| | Has Mastered | Beginning to Master |
|---|---|---|

**II. COGNITIVE DEVELOPMENT**

A.  Responds to or gives first name upon request _____ _____

B.  Points to or names one or more colors _____ _____

C.  Points to or names two or more body parts _____ _____

D.  Follows one-command directions (e.g., "Pick up the ball.") _____ _____

E.  Shows understanding of the purpose of objects (e.g., feeds doll with bottle or makes automobile noises while pushing toy car) _____ _____

F.  Experiments with toys and other objects (e.g., attempts to insert pieces into shapes toy) _____ _____

G.  Has age-appropriate attention span _____ _____

H.  Recalls some events or activities, such as when asked, "What did you eat?" _____ _____

I.  Explores new play spaces and materials _____ _____

J.  Enjoys a variety of textures (e.g., sand, water, play dough, paste) _____ _____

COMMENTS _____

_____

_____

_____

HOME STRATEGIES _____

_____

_____

_____

# CHILD PROGRESS REPORT
## (continued)

CHILD'S NAME _____ Date _____

| | Has Mastered | Beginning to Master |
|---|:---:|:---:|
| **III. LANGUAGE DEVELOPMENT** | | |
| A. Responds when name is called | _____ | _____ |
| B. Says simple words or short sentences | _____ | _____ |
| C. Names familiar objects when they are pointed to | _____ | _____ |
| D. Follows one-command directions (e.g., "Bring me the book.") | _____ | _____ |
| E. Verbalizes to adults and children | _____ | _____ |
| F. Vocalizations are usually understandable | _____ | _____ |
| G. Listens attentively to short stories | _____ | _____ |
| H. Points to pictures and vocalizes | _____ | _____ |
| I. Recognizes familiar sounds (e.g., such as responding to the ringing of the toy phone) | _____ | _____ |
| J. Participates in simple finger games | _____ | _____ |
| K. Attempts to say the names of others | _____ | _____ |

COMMENTS _____

_____

_____

_____

HOME STRATEGIES _____

_____

_____

_____

# CHILD PROGRESS REPORT
## (continued)

CHILD'S NAME _____ Date _____

| | Has Mastered | Beginning to Master |
|---|---|---|
| **IV. SOCIAL SKILLS** | | |
| A. Plays alone | _____ | _____ |
| B. Plays alongside of other children | _____ | _____ |
| C. Shows ownership of toys and materials | _____ | _____ |
| D. Seeks adult attention | _____ | _____ |
| E. Sometimes shares adult attention | _____ | _____ |
| F. Sometimes waits a short time for a turn | _____ | _____ |
| G. Imitates adult behavior | _____ | _____ |
| H. Occasionally follows simple classroom rules (e.g., "Please sit in your seat.") | _____ | _____ |

COMMENTS _____

_____

_____

_____

_____

_____

HOME STRATEGIES _____

_____

_____

_____

_____

_____

# CHILD PROGRESS REPORT
## (continued)

CHILD'S NAME _____ Date _____

| V.  EMOTIONAL DEVELOPMENT | Has Mastered | Beginning to Master |
|---|---|---|
| A. Sometimes cries when separating from parent(s) | _____ | _____ |
| B. Is calmed or comforted by a familiar adult | _____ | _____ |
| C. Seeks adults when fearful or uncertain | _____ | _____ |
| D. Is normally apprehensive around strangers | _____ | _____ |
| E. Expresses a broad range of emotions | _____ | _____ |
| F. Expresses affection for adults | _____ | _____ |
| G. Attaches to another adult (not a parent) who is a frequent caregiver | _____ | _____ |
| H. Shows interest in other children | _____ | _____ |
| I. Expresses hostility or anger toward others | _____ | _____ |
| J. Expresses needs, likes, and dislikes | _____ | _____ |
| K. Recognizes self in photograph or mirror | _____ | _____ |
| L. Shows pride or pleasure when praised | _____ | _____ |

COMMENTS _____

_____

_____

_____

HOME STRATEGIES _____

_____

_____

_____

# CHILD PROGRESS REPORT
## (continued)

CHILD'S NAME _____ Date _____

| | Has Mastered | Beginning to Master |
|---|---|---|
| **VI. SELF-HELP SKILLS** | | |
| A. Feeds self using fingers or utensils | _____ | _____ |
| B. Drinks from a cup | _____ | _____ |
| C. Sometimes indicates toileting needs (may be verbal or nonverbal) | _____ | _____ |
| D. Tries to wash own hands | _____ | _____ |
| E. Wipes mouth with napkin at mealtime | _____ | _____ |
| F. Attempts to put on coat or sweater | _____ | _____ |

COMMENTS _____
_____
_____
_____

HOME STRATEGIES _____
_____
_____
_____

SCHOOL STRATEGIES _____
_____
_____
_____
_____

# REMINDER ABOUT POLICY: FEES

**Child Care Center**

Dear _____:

    This is a reminder that fees for child care services are due and must be in the Center Director's office by _____. As you rely on our services, we also depend upon regular fee payments in order to operate the Program.

    If there are extenuating circumstances, please advise us, so that alternate payment arrangements can be explored. Otherwise, I will expect payment of the child care fees due no later than _____.

    We appreciate your prompt attention to this matter.

Sincerely,


_____

Center Director

# REMINDER ABOUT POLICY: MISSING RECORDS

Dear _____:

   A review of your child's records at the Center indicates that we are missing information about _____. State and Center policies require that our records be complete. Please bring this information to the Center no later than _____.

   Thank you for your compliance with this policy.

Sincerely,


_____
Center Director

# REMINDER ABOUT POLICY: SICK CHILD

**Child Care Center**

Dear _____:

On _____, immediately after your child was dropped off at the Center, staff found that _____ was ill with _____. Your child seemed quite ill, and staff contacted _____ to arrange a pick-up.

We are aware that making last-minute child care arrangements for a sick child can be difficult. However, the Center's policies regarding admittance of sick children, as stated in the *Parents' Handbook*, are very firm. These policies are designed to protect everyone from communicable illness. It is always better for all concerned if the sick child is absent from the Center until given clearance to return by a pediatrician or family doctor.

We hope that _____ is feeling better today, and look forward to having your child back at the Center soon. Please bring a copy of the physician clearance on return to the Center.

Thank you for your cooperation in this matter.

Sincerely,

_____
Center Director

# REMINDER ABOUT POLICY: LATENESS

Child Care Center

Dear _____:

    It has come to my attention that you have picked up your child after Center closing on _____ occasion(s). As stated in the *Parents' Handbook*, the Center closes at _____ promptly. It is important that a parent, or other previously designated adult, be present to pick up the child by that time. Accordingly, your next fee statement will reflect _____ in late pickup charges.

    Although circumstances may arise causing an occasional late pickup, parents are expected to contact the Center and to make alternate arrangements to assure that someone arrives to escort the child home by closing time.

    We appreciate your cooperation in this matter and look forward to continuing to provide services for your family.

Sincerely,

_____

Center Director

# REMINDER ABOUT POLICY: EMERGENCY CONTACTS

Dear _____:

　　As you know, on _____, the Center was forced to close early due to inclement weather. Staff attempted to contact you at your workplace. When we were unable to reach you, we called the list of emergency contacts provided by you when your child was admitted. Staff found, however, that none of the emergency contacts could be reached.

　　Center policy, as addressed in the *Parents' Handbook*, states that a minimum of three contacts, other than parents, must be on file with the Center. These must be individuals who can be reached if a parent is unavailable to pick up the child. Please use the attached slip to update the emergency contact information, and return it to the Center no later than _____.

　　Thank you for your cooperation in this matter.

Sincerely,


_____

Center Director

- - - - - - - - - - - - - - - - - - - - - - - - - -

### Emergency Contacts

　　The following are emergency contacts for _____ and are able
(child's name)
and willing to pick up my child when we are unavailable.

1. _____  _____  _____  _____
　　full name　　　　　　address　　　　　　telephone　　　　　relationship

2. _____  _____  _____  _____
　　full name　　　　　　address　　　　　　telephone　　　　　relationship

3. _____  _____  _____  _____
　　full name　　　　　　address　　　　　　telephone　　　　　relationship

Parent's/Guardian's Signature _____ Date _____

# REMINDER ABOUT POLICY: ADVISING CENTER OF CUSTODY CHANGE

## Child Care Center

Dear _____:

    You recently indicated to your child's teacher that you have been granted full custody of your child, and that your spouse is no longer permitted to pick up your child from the Center.

    In a situation such as this, the Center must be provided with a copy of the court order regarding custody. Without the court order, we cannot prohibit a parent from contact with your child in the event that he or she comes to the Center.

    We are anxious to support you and your family during this time. Please provide us with a copy of the custody order at your earliest convenience.

    Thank you for your cooperation in this matter.

Sincerely,


_____

Center Director

# REMINDER ABOUT POLICY: CHANGE OF ADDRESS/TELEPHONE NUMBER

Dear Parents:

    Please be advised that any time you change residence and/or telephone number, you must inform the Center immediately and complete the required form (available in the main office). A copy of this form is included below.

    Thank you for your consideration in this matter.

Sincerely,

_____

Center Director

- - - - - - - - - - - - - - - - - - - - - - - - - - - - - - - - -

**Family Change of Address/Telephone Number Form**

Family Name _____ Child _____

Previous Address _____

_____ Telephone _____

New Address _____

_____ Telephone _____

# CONGRATULATIONS: BIRTH OF A CHILD

Dear _____ Family:

Congratulations on the birth of your baby _____.
_____ has not stopped talking about the new addition to your family. _____ is so excited! We have been reading stories in the classroom about families expecting new babies and the changes that they bring. We know that your child will be a wonderful big (_brother/sister_).

When time permits, please bring the new baby for a visit. All the children and the staff are anxious to welcome your baby.

Our best wishes to you all.

Sincerely,

_____
Center Director

# CONGRATULATIONS: FAMILY WEDDING

Dear _____:

Thank you for sharing with us the news of your forthcoming wedding. I know that your child is very happy about your expanding family. (_He/She_) has been sharing the details of the ceremony and reception with teachers and the other children.

Congratulations! We wish you every happiness in your new life together.

Sincerely,

_____

Center Director

# ADOPTION OF A CHILD

Dear _____ Family:

Our sincere congratulations to you on the finalization of your adoption of _____. You are blessed to have such a dear child in your lives, and this child is lucky to have found such fine parents.

Adoption will certainly mean an adjustment for you all, and if the Center staff can provide any assistance, please call on us. Best wishes to you all.

Sincerely,


_____
Center Director

# CONDOLENCE

Dear _____ Family:

    All of the Center staff were saddened to learn of the recent death of _____. We have appreciated your efforts to keep us informed of the situation at home. We know that your child has been affected by this loss, and we will make every attempt to support (*him/her*) as (*he/she*) makes adjustments.

    Please advise us if the staff can be helpful to you. You are in our thoughts.

Sincerely,

_____

Center Director

# REQUEST FOR SUPPORT: FIELD TRIP

**Child Care Center**

Dear Parents:

On _____ the staff and children will spend the day at _____. This is a wonderful place for children with a variety of age-appropriate attractions.

In order to maximize the children's safety and enjoyment on this outing, we need the assistance of parents who can spend the day with us. There is no cost to parents for bus transportation, and lunch will be provided by the Center. Buses will depart from the Center at _____ and will return to the Center at _____.

If your schedule can be arranged to join us on this trip, please sign the Trip Volunteers' Sign-Up Sheet in your child's classroom, or telephone the Center at _____ no later than _____. If you have any questions about the trip, a staff member or I are available to answer them for you.

We hope that you can join us!

Sincerely,

_____

Center Director

# REQUEST FOR SUPPORT: MATERIALS

Dear Parents:

On behalf of the Center staff, we genuinely appreciate the many ways that you contribute to our program. It is through your involvement that we are able to provide quality services to your child.

In order to further enhance our curriculum, we need many types of materials. Many of these are purchased with funds from our budget, but many other items come to us as donations. Below you will find a list of items that are regularly needed by the teachers and are used in our work with the children. If you have access to and can donate any of these items, please bring them to the Center and leave them in the main office.

Thank you once again for your support!

Sincerely,

_____

Center Director

Items needed in Center classrooms include:

- baby food jars
- margarine containers with lids
- toilet and paper towel rolls
- used computer paper (blank on one side)
- empty computer paper boxes with lids
- Styrofoam trays
- plastic gallon milk containers
- two-liter plastic soda bottles
- clear Con-Tact® paper
- washable scarves, elastic-waist skirts, shirts, and ties
- newspaper
- extra sets of clean children's clothing: shirts, pants, socks (sizes 2, 4, 5, 6, 7)

© 2002 by The Center for Applied Research in Education

# PARENT CONFLICT WITH STAFF MEMBER

Dear _____:

Thank you for your telephone call informing me of the conversation that you had with _____, your child's teacher. I understand you have some concerns regarding this conversation and/or events at the Center.

Rest assured that I will sit down to discuss the situation with _____ today. If you would like to meet briefly with _____ and me on _____ when you pick up your child, I am sure that we can prevent any further miscommunications. Please call me at _____ to let me know if the meeting time is convenient for you.

We look forward to continuing to work with you and your child.

Sincerely,


_____

Center Director

# THANK-YOU FOR INFORMATION ABOUT A CHILD

## Child Care Center

Dear _____:

    Thank you for the information regarding your child's recent health problem. I know that we have all been concerned about (_him/her_), and it is a great relief to know the nature of (_his/her_) problem. Rest assured that the staff will carefully follow the instructions provided by Dr. _____ regarding your child's care and administration of medications.

    If there are any changes in instructions regarding the medications or treatment, please advise us immediately. As your family makes adjustments to coping with _____, I am sure that there will be many questions. Please do not hesitate to contact us at _____ if there is any information that we can provide.

Sincerely,


_____

Center Director

# THANK-YOU TO FIELD-TRIP VOLUNTEER

**Child Care Center**

Dear _____ :

    Thank you for taking time from your busy schedule to accompany the children and staff on the trip to _____. Your child was clearly delighted to have (*his/her*) _____ along on the trip. We noted that you also took time to be attentive to many of the other children.

    When parents/guardians volunteer as you so often do, not only is the trip a safer activity, but all the adults participate in creating more learning opportunities for the children. I hope that it was an enjoyable day for your child and for you.

Sincerely,

_____

Center Director

# THANK-YOU FOR DONATION OF MATERIALS

## Child Care Center

Dear _____:

    Staff members were so delighted by your response to our recent request for curriculum materials ! These materials will be utilized in many upcoming activities for the children.

    I would like to take this opportunity to thank you for the many times that you have responded to our requests for parent involvement. Your commitment to your child's care and education, and willingness to support our efforts, provide us with encouragement to continue our efforts as teachers.

    Thank you again for your many contributions to our program.

Sincerely,


_____

Center Director

# THANK-YOU FOR ASSISTANCE WITH HOME–SCHOOL EVENT

Dear _____:

    It is with thanks to parents like yourselves that our recent Thanksgiving Feast was such a huge success! I appreciate the time you took to prepare the many tasty and nutritious side dishes that you shared with our families. _____ fairly beamed with pride as she pointed out to her friends the foods that you had contributed to our meal.

    I am certain that I speak for everyone who attended the Feast when I say "Great job!"

Sincerely,

_____

Center Director

# CONCERN FOR CHILD: CHANGE IN BEHAVIOR

## Child Care Center

Dear _____:

    I am hoping that your schedule(s) will permit you to meet with your child's teacher and me one day next week. The staff has noticed several changes in your child's behavior during the past few weeks, as well as reluctance to participate in play and activities in the usual ways.

    Your little one has always been such a happy child, and we enjoy having (*him/her*) at the Center. Staff members are concerned that we may be missing some way to help your child feel more comfortable during the school day. Please contact me at _____ to make an appointment convenient for you. I am certain that together we can identify ways to help your child.

Sincerely,


_____

Center Director

# CONCERN FOR CHILD: IDENTIFYING SPECIAL NEEDS

Dear _____:

I am aware that your child's teacher recently met with you about scheduling an appointment for your daughter with an audiologist. I imagine that you must be feeling some concern. As you know, our staff has noticed that your child does not always respond when her name is called, and she seems to be having difficulty following stories and learning new songs. These things represent a change in her usual behavior. Sometimes they are indicators that a child is not hearing as well as she should. Since your child had a series of ear infections during the winter months, there could be a relationship between these and the changes noticed by our teachers.

No one on our staff at the Center is qualified to test your child's hearing, and this is why we recommend scheduling an appointment for screening at the Audiology Clinic. Staff there are trained to work with young children. The tests are not painful, and if your child has any hearing problem, it is likely that she can be treated. The number at the Clinic is _____.

Please contact me at _____ when you have received the results of the hearing screening. We look forward to continuing to work with you and with your child.

Sincerely,


_____
Center Director

# TRIP PERMISSION

Dear Parents:

The children will be participating in a field trip described below. Please indicate your permission for your child to attend the trip by signing and returning the attached slip.

Thank you for your cooperation in this matter.

Sincerely,

_____

Center Director

– – – – – – – – – – – – – – – – – – – – – – – – – – – – – – –

**Permission Slip**

Trip location: _____

Trip date: _____

Fee for trip: _____

Lunch supplied: _____

Trip departure time: _____

Return time: _____

Transportation by: _____

Permission due by: _____

I give permission for my child, _____, to accompany his or her class on the trip described above.

Parent's/Guardian's Signature _____ Date _____

# INVITATION TO EVENT: PARENTS' MEETING

Dear Parents:

The monthly meeting of our Parents' Group is scheduled for _____ from _____ until _____. After the business portion of our meeting is concluded, Dr. Laura Brown from the Community College of Philadelphia will lead a discussion on "Helping Young Children Develop Appropriate Behaviors."

Child care provided by the Center staff is available until _____, and a potluck dinner is planned. If you can contribute a covered dish for the meeting, please let _____ in Room _____ know what you will be bringing. Covered dishes can be dropped off on _____ morning, and the meal will be ready when you arrive for the meeting.

We look forward to your input at our Parents' Group gathering!

Sincerely,


_____

Center Director

# INVITATION TO EVENT: THANKSGIVING FEAST

Dear Parents and Family Members:

On Wednesday, November 23, beginning at noon, the Center will host the annual Thanksgiving Feast. This is a family activity, and on behalf of the children, teachers, and other staff, I cordially invite you to come and share a meal with us. The Feast is open to parents/guardians, grandparents, and siblings of children who attend the Center.

This is a very special day for the children and staff. During the week prior to the Feast, children will clean and decorate the Center in preparation for the visit by their family members.

The Center will supply turkeys, paper goods, cold drinks, and desserts. Your contributions of side dishes are needed to complete the meal. Some suggested side dishes are listed below. Your ideas are welcome.

- stuffing
- corn pudding
- green beans
- sweet potatoes
- green salad (dressings on the side)
- collard greens
- macaroni and cheese
- cole slaw
- scalloped potatoes
- rolls

If you will be contributing a dish for the Thanksgiving Feast, please telephone the Center at _____ to advise us. We look forward to celebrating the holiday with you.

Sincerely,

_____

Center Director

- - - - - - - - - - - - - - - - - - - - - - - - - - - - - -

I (*circle one*) will/will not attend the Thanksgiving Feast on November 23. I will contribute _____ for the feast.

Parent's/Guardian's Signature _____ Date _____

© 2002 by The Center for Applied Research in Education

# INVITATION TO EVENT: JULY 4th PICNIC

Dear Parents:

I am pleased to announce a Center-sponsored July 4th picnic trip to _____. Children attending the Center, their siblings, parents, and grandparents are invited to join us for a day of barbecuing, rides, and games. Buses will leave the Center promptly at _____, and will return to the Center at _____. All children must be accompanied by a parent or related adult over age 18, who is expected to take charge of that child. This is not a work day for the staff, and they will have no child care responsibilities during the trip.

The Center will supply hot dogs, hamburgers, rolls, condiments, sodas, and paper goods. The _____ provides barbecue grills, which we will reserve in advance. A family that plans to do its own barbecuing should contact _____ to reserve a grill.

We are requesting donations of side dishes from parents. Suggested dishes are listed below. If you contribute a dish requiring refrigeration, please bring an ice chest or cooler to store the dish.

If you are planning to accompany us on the picnic trip, please contact the Center at _____ with the number of children and adults and the side dish that you will contribute. We are expecting a clear, hot day and loads of fun for the entire family. Come and join us on July 4th.

Sincerely,

_____

Center Director

Suggested contributions for the July 4th picnic:

- baked beans
- potato chips
- green salad (dressings on the side)
- macaroni salad
- pickles
- cupcakes

- pretzels
- deviled eggs
- cole slaw
- tuna salad
- fruit salad
- corn on the cob

# INVITATION TO EVENT: GRADUATION CEREMONY

Dear Families:

I cherish fond memories as I spend time writing a letter like this one. During the past years, I have watched your children grow physically as well as socially and emotionally. Now, it is time to bid them farewell as they prepare to leave our program. Therefore, the staff, Board members, and I are pleased to request the honor of your presence at our upcoming graduation ceremony.

The ceremony will take place on _____ at _____ at the Center. You are invited to bring siblings, relatives, and guests to share this happy occasion with you. A reception will follow the ceremony. In order for us to accommodate all families and their guests, please fill out the form below and drop it off with your child's teacher before _____.

We look forward to seeing you on this very happy occasion.

Sincerely,


_____

Center Director

- - - - - - - - - - - - - - - - - - - - - - - - -

Name of Child _____

Number of Guests _____

Special Accommodations for Any Guest

_____

_____


Please return this form before _____ to your child's teacher.

© 2002 by The Center for Applied Research in Education

FIGURE 1.4

# INVITATION TO EVENT: GRADUATION CEREMONY ANNOUNCEMENT

You are cordially invited to attend

Graduation Ceremonies

for the

Class of _____ of the

_____
Center Name

at

_____ o'clock p.m.

at

_____

Reception to follow

# INVITATION TO EVENT: GRANDPARENTS' DAY

*Grandparents' Day*

Dear Families:

_____ is the national observance of Grandparents' Day. Knowing how important grandparents and other mature adults are in the lives of our children, we are having a special celebration at the Center.

Children will be making invitations to give to their grandparents or other close adult. These invitations will invite grandparents to share lunch with the children at the Center on Grandparents' Day. The children will assist in making and serving the lunch, and will make party favors for their guests.

We hope that there is a special adult in your child's life who will attend our Grandparents' Day festivities.

Sincerely,

_____

Center Director

# SHARED INFORMATION

Dear _____:

Thank you for sharing with me the story of the recent loss of your mother. I know that her illness had a profound impact on your family, and I admire the way that you and your family pulled together and included your child during such a stressful time.

As we discussed, there are many local groups designed to assist grieving families. Support from others also experiencing a loss can be helpful to some people. A family grief group meets on _____ at _____ at _____. No appointment is needed to attend, and there is no obligation to attend additional meetings.

Please let me or a member of the staff know if we can assist you or your family in any way. You are in our thoughts.

Sincerely,


_____
Center Director

# CHILD UPDATE #1

## Child Care Center

Dear _____:

    I am so pleased to report that your child is doing exceptionally well at the Center since the surgery to put the tubes into his ears. Your quick response to our shared concerns about his hearing has resulted in a positive change in your son's language development. Your child is once again participating fully in activities, singing songs, and discussing stories and events with the other children.

    As we discussed previously, the speech therapist will continue to work with your child three times each week until _____. She will be providing you with a monthly report on your child's skills improvement. Please contact me at _____ if you have any further questions or input regarding these plans for your child.

Sincerely,


_____
Center Director

# CHILD UPDATE #2

## Child Care Center

Dear _____:

Since our _____ meeting with you, staff have made a concerted effort to follow the plan we developed to help your child express her anger in more appropriate ways. I know that you are very concerned about your child and have also tried to apply the plan in your home.

Since our mutual efforts do not seem to be benefiting your child, I would like to recommend that we call in Dr. _____ to assist us. Dr. _____ is a child psychologist with excellent credentials. Over the years she has helped several children attending the Center to cope with difficult issues.

With permission from a child's parents, the doctor observes a child over several weeks, and gathers information about the child from the parents and the staff who work directly with the child. All gathered information is held in the strictest confidence. Finally, she makes recommendations to the parent for helping the child. Of course, we hope that these will be shared with the staff who work with the child. There is no charge for her services.

If you are interested in having Dr. _____ observe and develop a plan for your child, please call me at the Center at _____. I can also make arrangements for you to talk directly with the doctor before you make your decision.

I look forward to talking with you soon.

Sincerely,


_____
Center Director

# FAREWELL TO FAMILY

Dear _____ Family:

It is hard to believe that you and your child will soon be moving to _____. I remember clearly when you first enrolled _____ in the Center. Soon she will be ready to begin kindergarten in a new school and in a new town.

It has been a great pleasure working with you and your child. We have been through some interesting challenges together, but your clear devotion to your child and willingness to work with her teachers will put you both in good stead as she moves through childhood, wherever you go.

Please keep in touch with the Center, and let us know how your family is adjusting in your new home. Very best wishes from all the Center's families and staff as you begin your new life!

Sincerely,


_____

Center Director

# DATE DUE: CHILD'S ANNUAL PHYSICAL

Dear Parents:

As per the information found in the Parents' Handbook, annual physical exams for children admitted to the Center on or before _____ are due in the Center Director's office no later than _____. Please check your weekly fee receipt for the anniversary date of your child's admission to the Center. Physical examination forms, to be completed by a pediatrician or family physician, are located in the pockets outside of each classroom door.

Maintaining up-to-date child health records is an important obligation of the Center administration, and inaccurate records can affect renewal of the Center's license. If a child's records have not been updated by _____, he or she will not be admitted for child care services until a current record is on file.

Thank you for your cooperation in this matter.

Sincerely,


_____

Center Director

# DATE DUE: FIELD-TRIP FEE

## Child Care Center

Dear Parents:

A reminder to parents/guardians of children who will be taking the Center-sponsored trip to the _____ on _____, that the trip fee (for transportation, admission, and lunch) of _____ is due by _____. Fees should be given by a parent/guardian to your child's teacher in cash. Checks will not be accepted, and teachers cannot inspect children's backpacks for envelopes. Teachers will note the fees received in a log kept in the classroom.

The program will continue at the Center for those children not participating in the field trip.

Thank you for your cooperation in this matter.

Sincerely,

_____

Center Director

# DISMISSAL FROM THE PROGRAM

Dear ——————————————:

In spite of our recent attempts to talk with you by telephone, and registered letters reminding you about Center policies regarding lateness, you have continued to arrive at the Center after closing time to pick up your child. Staff members are not equipped or expected to be responsible for children after Center closing hours.

Although we would have liked to work with you toward a resolution of this issue, you have been unavailable for several weeks. Therefore, I am forced to terminate child care services for your children effective today, ——————————.

It is essential that Center policies be observed by parents. This decision is final and not open to appeal. I will expect payment for services provided on Monday, Tuesday, and Wednesday to be paid no later than ——————————.

Sincerely,


_____

Center Director

# REPORT OF AN ACCIDENT

Dear _____:

Today _____, your child, _____, _____
          (date)                ( child's name)     (description of accident)

_____. Your child suffered _____

_____.
              (description of injury)

Following the accident, a staff member _____
                             (description of treatment)

_____.

Please contact me at _____ if I can provide any further information about this incident.

Sincerely,


_____
Center Director

© 2002 by The Center for Applied Research in Education

# REPORT OF AN INCIDENT

## Child Care Center

Dear Parents:

    I am writing to tell you of an incident that occurred at the Center on _____ at _____. At that time _____

_____

_____

_____

_____

_____

_____

_____

    Be assured that staff and other authorities are handling this situation with care. When further information becomes available, I will provide it to the Center families and staff. If I can answer any questions about this event, please contact me at the Center at _____. It is important that any information shared be factual.

Sincerely,


_____

Center Director

# PARENT OF THE MONTH

Dear _____:

  In recognition of your service to the Center, especially the work that you contributed to _____, the Center Advisory Board has named you Parent of the Month. Please accept the enclosed certificate as a small token of our appreciation for your contributions to our program! It is the generosity and dedication of parents that make the work of staff easier and have made our Center the caring place it is.

Sincerely,

_____

Center Director

FIGURE 1.5

## PARENT-OF-THE-MONTH
## CERTIFICATE

FIGURE 1.6

# PARENT-VOLUNTEER CERTIFICATE

## Parent Volunteer

Teacher

Director

# Letters and Certificates for Children

You might well ask the question, "Why bother to include a section on letters and certificates for children who are too young to read?" The answer is simple: because children care, even as young as 18 months of age, about getting their own mail or a special document that parents will display at home. Writing to children or rewarding them with a certificate plays a vital role in educating both parents and children.

When we write to children, we tell the entire family that the child is valued. The child feels important, and so do the parents. The family's esteem is elevated and their bond with their child is enhanced by the simple act of writing and mailing a letter. Many early childhood education programs now include writing interest centers, where children can experiment with "writing, stamping, and mailing" letters of their own. Children see that their parents receive mail, and enjoy getting their own mail.

Parents are able to observe the impact of letters and certificates on their child. They will come to understand that letters and awards are a way of rewarding and supporting their children, and they may even incorporate these into their parenting.

Sending letters and award certificates to children also supports the growth of family literacy. Children will ask parents again and again, "What does it say?" Parents can proudly read and reread the letter or certificate to their child, and thus support the child's interest in printed matter.

Some people have suggested that, with the popularity of computers, letter writing is a dying art. They suggest that one day written communication will be only by e-mail. We certainly hope not! There is a great joy in penning your own letters, in selecting special paper to write them on, in stamping them and taking them to the mailbox, and in waiting for a reply. Part of learning to communicate effectively involves experiencing the pleasures of writing and receiving letters.

# WELCOME TO SCHOOL

Dear _____,

We are so glad that you and your parents have chosen our school, and we are looking forward to seeing you on _____.

Your new teacher is _____. Your classroom is _____. Some of your friends at the Center are _____ and _____. They want to show you all around your new classroom. There are many toys and books and other activities that you will enjoy.

We will see you soon.

Your friend,

_____

# HAPPY BIRTHDAY

Dear _____,

It is your special day. Today you are _____
years old!

Your friends at the Center are planning a party to
celebrate. We will have treats and a birthday cake. We
hope you will have a happy birthday!

Your friend,

_____

FIGURE 2.1

# HAPPY-BIRTHDAY CERTIFICATE

# SICK CHILD

Dear _____,

All of your friends at the Center are sad to know that you are not feeling well. We think about you often, and the children have made cards to let you know that they miss you.

We hope that you are taking your medicine and doing everything that your parents and the doctor ask you to do.

Feel better soon!

Your friend,

_____

# NEW BROTHER OR SISTER

Dear _____,

So, you have a new baby at your house! That is exciting news! Do you remember all of the books that we read at school about babies? When you come back to school, you must tell us if your baby does all of the things that the babies in the books do. Does your baby cry and sleep and wet a diaper? Does your baby eat a lot? What is your baby's name?

We can't wait to find out more about your baby! Please bring a picture of your baby to school.

Your friend,

_____

FIGURE 2.2

# BIG-BROTHER CERTIFICATE

Big Brother

Director

Teacher

FIGURE 2.3

# BIG-SISTER CERTIFICATE

# IMPROVED BEHAVIOR

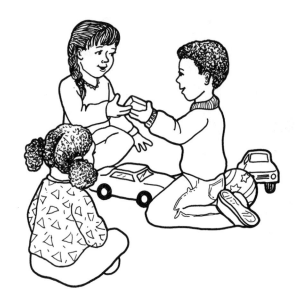

Dear _____,

I just wanted to let you know what a good person you have been at school. I know that you are working hard to wait for your turn, and to stay in your chair at snack and lunch time. You are doing a great job.

All of your friends are proud of you!

Your friend,

_____

# HELPFUL TO OTHER CHILDREN

Dear _____,

All of the teachers have noticed how kind and helpful you are to the other children. You always share your toys and wait for your turn during activities. When other children have trouble with their projects, you are always there to help them.

We are glad to have such a kind friend at our school!

Your friend,

_____

FIGURE 2.4

# GOOD-FRIEND CERTIFICATE

# CHANGING SCHOOLS

Dear _____,

Your parents have told us that you will soon be going to a new school. We will miss you very much, but we know that you will make many new friends and have great adventures.

Please write to us and tell us all about your new school, and we will write letters to you.

Have fun at your new school!

Your friend,

_____

# GOING TO KINDERGARTEN

Dear _____,

It is hard to believe that you have become a kindergartner! We remember when you were just a little person, and now you are on your way to a new grade and a new school.

Some of the other children from our Center will also start kindergarten, so you will have friends at your new school. You will also make new friends and meet new teachers. Perhaps you would like to visit us one day with your parents and tell the other children about your kindergarten class. Have fun!

Your friend,

_____

FIGURE 2.5

# PRESCHOOL-GRADUATE
# CERTIFICATE

# PARENT'S GRADUATION

Dear _____,

Congratulations on your _____
graduation from _____! You must be
proud because a parent cannot graduate unless their
child helps them. You must have been a good helper at
home.

Please ask your _____ to bring the
graduation diploma to the Center so that all the
children can see it.

Your friend,

_____

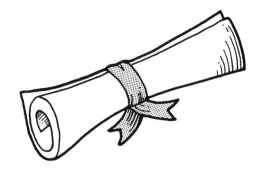

# HELPER AWARD

Dear _____,

Congratulations! You are the Helper of the Month at _____ for the month of _____ because you have worked very hard at school. You will be able to help your teacher with all of the activities and lead the lines to go outside.

Good job!

Your friend,

_____

FIGURE 2.6

# HELPER-OF-THE-MONTH
## CERTIFICATE

Helper of the Month

Director

Teacher

# Letters to Teachers and Staff

An early childhood education leader assumes many important responsibilities. Among these are the development and implementation of programs for children and their families. Equally significant is the role played as a supervisor of staff. In this capacity, a center director must review and screen applications to fill positions; communicate and implement policy and procedures; resolve grievances; and support a range of staff needs. On the occasions when there have been serious violations of policy, a director must sometimes terminate staff.

In the role of leader, an early childhood educator deals with many of the same issues faced by the vanguard in other professions. A leader assures that staff understand the primary mission of the agency, and follow plans designed to address those aims. Staff must feel that they are given the option of contributing their ideas toward the improvement and success of the program. While in some sense, no individual is more significant than the agency's goals, at the same time, staff must be treated as the individuals that they are. Their unique talents, needs, life circumstances, and families must be handled with respect and consideration. A director must provide praise, support, and nurturance as those distinctive qualities demand.

The responsibilities of staff must be clearly outlined, along with the lines of authority. When staff encounter situations plainly outside their authority, or when problems arise that create uncertainty regarding the chain of command, staff must know when and how to consult a supervisor. Furthermore, respect for a director's position should not be coupled with fear of reprisal for daring to voice a concern, for suggesting a programmatic improvement, or for requesting assistance.

An early childhood education director has an ongoing responsibility to mentor those staff under his or her supervision. As a mentor, the director regularly evaluates staff and provides feedback for professional growth. Staff should expect to receive support for continuing education, for appropriate expansion of their roles, and for eventual pursuit of career advancement.

Finally, directors must see themselves in the capacity of learners. While some of us may be born leaders with an inherent ability to command others, none of us has the capacity to know all. The best leaders learn from those around them, know how to delegate responsibility, and support the special skills of those they mentor. Over the course of time, they become better at what they do because they are watching, listening to, and are enriched by those around them.

# WELCOME BACK TO SCHOOL

Dear Staff Members:

Welcome back to school! I hope that you enjoyed a restful and stress-free holiday. As we prepare for the return of the children, a few reminders:

- Classrooms and restrooms have been thoroughly cleaned and the floors waxed. Furniture has been returned to the place it was in prior to vacation. If assistance is required to rearrange furniture, please notify me so that I can ask _____, our maintenance engineer, for help.

- Materials and equipment have been ordered for each classroom and are due in the upcoming week. As you unpack supplies, please advise me of any missing items.

- The first set of activity plans is due _____. Please use the activity plan sheets available in the office for your plans.

- The first day for new children is _____, and returning children will be joining us on _____.

With your help, I am anticipating an exciting and rewarding school year. Please come to talk with me about any problems or concerns.

Thank you for all your efforts on behalf of our children and families.

Sincerely,

_____

Center Director

# INTRODUCTION
# TO *STAFF HANDBOOK*

Child Care Center

Dear Staff Member:

Welcome to _____! We are pleased to welcome you to our Center family. In the following pages, you will find descriptions of our Program philosophy; goals for children, parent, staff, and community involvement; job descriptions; holidays observed; and policies and procedures. During your required study of the *Staff Handbook*, you may have questions regarding employee requirements. If so, please visit the Center office for clarification.

Although work with young children and parents can be very challenging, it is some of the most rewarding work to be found. We have the opportunity to help the child and parents build a solid foundation for learning and understanding as they begin life together. It is important, however, that we share common ideals and goals, and that we move along similar paths to reach these aims. I am here to assist in this process and my door is always open to hear about your needs and concerns.

Thank you in advance for all the contributions you will make to the lives of our families, and to us all.

Sincerely,

_____

Center Director

# OPEN HOUSE

*You are Cordially Invited to an Open House*

Dear Staff Members:

On _____ from _____ until _____, the Center will host an Open House for community members and interested families. This is an opportunity to put our best face forward and promote the value and quality of our services while recruiting new clients. I have also invited the local television stations to be present, so we may be featured on local news. All staff are asked to participate in cleaning and preparing their respective spaces for this event. Children's art work should be used as decoration. Classrooms, restrooms, offices, and other spaces in the Center will be on public view.

Refreshments will be provided by the Center, and guests will be able to participate in classroom art, story, and music activities in each classroom. Planning for these activities will begin at our next regular staff meeting.

A reminder that lead teachers in each classroom will be asked to answer questions posed by our guests at the Open House. Other staff members are asked to refer questions to lead teachers or Center administration.

Working together, we can make the Open House a great success. Thank you in advance for your support of this event.

Sincerely,

_____
Center Director

# THANK-YOU FOR YOUR RÉSUMÉ

Child Care Center

Dear _____:

    We have received your résumé, sent in response to our advertisement for a classroom teacher in the _____. Interviews for this position are currently being scheduled, and you should be hearing from a member of our Hiring Committee in the near future.

    Our child care program offers comprehensive services for 50 children and their families. Some families are now sending a second generation of children to our Center. More than half of our staff have been employed at the Center for ten or more years. In addition to those qualifications listed in our advertisement, we are seeking an individual who will make a long-term commitment to our agency.

    Thank you for your interest in our child care center. We are looking forward to meeting you in the near future.

Sincerely,


_____
Center Director

# JOB DENIAL

## Child Care Center

Dear _____:

    Thank you for your résumé, submitted in response to our advertisement for a classroom teacher in the _____ room.

    While you have many accomplishments, at this time we do not have a position open that fits with your educational background and work experience. We will, however, keep your résumé on file for a period of six months and will contact you should a position be created that is relevant to your skills.

    Thank you for your interest in our child care center.

Sincerely,


_____

Center Director

# MORE INFORMATION NEEDED

Dear _____ :

    As per our telephone conversation, we are still awaiting the arrival of your official transcripts from the colleges you have attended. We enjoyed meeting you during the interview on _____, and would like to be able to consider your application for the position of _____ further. Once we have received your transcripts, we will contact you regarding our decision.

    If there is anything else that you would like to communicate and/or share with us regarding your qualifications for this position, please do not hesitate to contact us. You may write or call in the upcoming week at _____.

    Thank you for your interest in our program.

Sincerely,


_____

Center Director

# HIRING STAFF

## Child Care Center

Dear —————————————:

    The Hiring Committee for the child care center is pleased to offer you the position of ——————————————. The annual salary for this position is ——————————————, and employee benefits include life insurance as well as staff and dependent health-care coverage. A pension plan will be added to employee benefits in the upcoming year.

    As per our telephone conversation, the starting date for this position is ——————————. At that time you will fill out the paperwork and insurance forms required of all new hires. Please bring with you two proofs of United States citizenship (such as a birth certificate, driver's license, and passport), and current criminal history, child abuse, and health clearances.

    We are delighted to welcome you to our staff! I am certain that you will make an invaluable contribution to our program.

Sincerely,


————————————————

Center Director

FIGURE 3.1

# SAMPLE STAFF CONTRACT

This contract is made between _____
(center name)

hereafter known as the employer, and _____, hereafter
(staff name)

known as the employee. Whereas this employee is hired in the capacity

of _____ to work in the employer's child care
(job title)

center for a period of _____ from date of contract signature,
(length of contract)

working with preschool-age children and having responsibilities to

_____.
(description of duties)

In turn, the employer will provide an annual salary of _____
(salary)

for a forty-hour week, with compensatory time to be due in the event of

overtime hours. The employee further agrees to provide health, dental,

worker's compensation, and life insurance as described in the *Staff*

*Handbook.*


_____          _____

Employer's Signature              Employee's signature


_____          _____

Date                              Date

# POLICY MEMORANDUM #1:
# STAFF DRESS CODE

## Child Care Center

To:      Child Care Center Staff

From: Child Care Center Director

Re:      Staff Dress Code

Date: _____

As per the *Staff Handbook*, a reminder to all about the policy regarding dress considered appropriate for male and female staff while at work.

*Staff may wear slacks, skirts, or dresses while at the Center. No shorts, halters, or midriff-bearing tops are permitted. Sneakers or other low-heeled shoes are recommended. Staff working directly with children are not permitted to wear high-heeled shoes or open-toed sandals. Printed tee shirts may show only tastefully rendered graphics and designs.*

Thank you for your cooperation in this matter.

# POLICY MEMORANDUM #2:
# STAFF ATTENDANCE

**Child Care Center**

To:     Child Care Center Staff

From: Child Care Center Director

Re:     Staff Attendance

Date: _____

As per the *Staff Handbook*, a reminder to all about the policy regarding attendance at work.

*Staff are expected to arrive at the child care center on time for their scheduled shift. If unexpectedly detained en route to work, staff are expected to contact the Center. If unplanned absence arises, staff must contact the Center or Center Director at least two hours prior to the start of scheduled work times. Staff who fail to observe Center attendance policies may have missed time deducted from their weekly paycheck(s).*

Thank you for your cooperation in this matter.

# POLICY MEMORANDUM #3: RELATIONSHIPS WITH PARENTS

**Child Care Center**

To:     Child Care Center Staff

From:  Child Care Center Director

Re:     Home–School Relationships

Date:  _____

    As per the *Staff Handbook*, a reminder to all about the policy regarding home–school relationships.

*Staff are asked to be continuously mindful of the importance of positive relationships between the Center staff and children's families. Questions from parents about their children are to be directed to the teacher in charge of each classroom. Questions about children from adults other than their parents should be directed to the Center Director. Serious concerns posed by parents or other primary caretakers also should be brought to the attention of the Center Director. If conflicts arise between a staff member and a parent that cannot be immediately resolved, the Director should be advised and an intervention will be made.*

Thank you for your cooperation in this matter.

# POLICY MEMORANDUM #4: STAFF RELATIONSHIPS

To: Child Care Center Staff

From: Child Care Center Director

Re: Staff Relationships

Date: _____

As per the *Staff Handbook*, a reminder to all about the policy regarding staff relationships.

*Harmonious relationships between child care center staff are important to effective work with children and their families. Staff are expected to treat one another with respect and consideration at all times. If unresolvable or continuing conflicts arise between staff members, the Center Director is to be consulted. Inappropriate staff behavior (e.g., loud quarreling or physical altercations) may result in dismissal.*

Thank you for your cooperation in this matter.

# POLICY MEMORANDUM #5: CHILD-DISCIPLINE POLICIES

To:     Child Care Center Staff

From:   Child Care Center Director

Re:     Child-Discipline Policies

Date:   _____

As per the *Staff Handbook*, a reminder to all about the policy regarding child discipline.

*Staff are encouraged to help children develop appropriate behavior and display of emotions. At all times, staff are encouraged to remember that children are in the process of learning about adult expectations. When children's behavior is inappropriate, they may be removed from the area, may receive a time-out of no more than five minutes, or may be disallowed participation in an activity. Staff cannot reject any child's request for food, water, rest, or toilet time. At no time should any form of corporal punishment be used, including spanking, slapping, or pushing. Staff must also refrain from verbal abuse, including yelling at or embarrassing children. Violations of child-discipline policies may result in employee dismissal.*

*Policies concerning child discipline are important to the maintenance of high-quality care and education that is the philosophy of the agency. Any deviations from this policy are potentially damaging to children and to the goals of the Program.*

Thank you for your cooperation in this matter.

# POLICY MEMORANDUM #6:
# EMERGENCY CENTER CLOSINGS

To:     Child Care Center Staff

From:  Child Care Center Director

Re:     Emergency Center Closings

Date: _____

As per the *Staff Handbook*, a reminder to all about the policy regarding emergency closings of the Center.

*Decisions regarding closing of the child care center are to be made only by the Center Director or President of the Policy Board. The Center may be closed unexpectedly in the event of inclement weather or other unforeseen circumstance. Closings resulting from the weather will be announced on the Center's voice-mail announcement, as well as on local radio and television stations. If it becomes necessary to close the Center during the course of the school day, staff may be assigned responsibility for contacting children's parents and/or designated emergency contacts. In no case may a staff member assigned to close the Center leave before the last remaining child has been picked up by a responsible adult.*

Thank you for your cooperation in this matter.

# POLICY MEMORANDUM #7: MORNING HEALTH CHECKS

## Child Care Center

To:     Child Care Center Staff

From: Child Care Center Director

Re:     Morning Health Checks

Date: _____

As per the *Staff Handbook*, a reminder to all about the policy regarding children's morning health checks by staff.

*Upon arrival at the child care center each morning, each child should be visually checked by a staff member for signs of illness. The health check should include signs of: a flushed or feverish appearance; unusual discharge from eyes, ears, or nose; report of abdominal pain or headache; or vomiting or diarrhea. If signs of illness are observed, the parent or caregiver should be asked to find alternative care for the child for that day. If the parent has already departed the Program, staff should consult the emergency contact list and telephone a responsible adult to transport the child to his/her home.*

Daily health checks provide reasonable assurance that children arrive at the Center in good health and ready to start the day. These checks help to maintain the well-being of each child, the group, and the staff.

Thank you for your cooperation in this matter.

# POLICY MEMORANDUM #8: WEEKLY CURRICULUM PLANNING

**Child Care Center**

To:     Child Care Center Staff

From:  Child Care Center Director

Re:     Weekly Curriculum Planning

Date: _____

As per the *Staff Handbook*, a reminder to all about the policy regarding curriculum planning by staff.

*Staff in each classroom are to schedule a weekly meeting designed to plan the specific activities to be conducted in the upcoming week. Meetings can be held during the children's rest/nap times. Plans are to be recorded on the Activity Plan Sheets available in the main office, and must be kept on file in each classroom where they will be shared with substitute staff as needed.*

*Activity Plan Sheets provide a record of the curriculum that is useful for evaluation and future planning, and are used by substitutes when teachers are absent.*

Thank you for your cooperation in this matter.

FIGURE 3.2

# ACTIVITY PLAN SHEET

Staff Name _____ Date Submitted _____

Name of Activity _____
(e.g., Making Bread)

Related Theme or Skill Area _____
(e.g., Foods that Are Good for Me)

**Purpose of the Activity** (e.g., learning about nutritious foods/to prepare nutritious foods; developing cooperation; learning about measurement; developing sequencing skills; developing vocabulary)

_____

_____

Ages of children _____ Number in group _____
(e.g., small group/whole class)

Materials needed _____

_____

**Procedures to Be Followed** (A step-by-step description; include the way the activity is introduced, roles of teacher and children, and the way the activity is ended.)

_____

_____

_____

_____

_____

**Evaluation** _____

_____

_____

_____

_____

_____

# POLICY MEMORANDUM #9: BIWEEKLY STAFF MEETINGS

To:     Child Care Center Staff

From:   Child Care Center Director

Re:     Biweekly Staff Meetings

Date:   _____

    As per the *Staff Handbook,* a reminder to all about the policy regarding biweekly staff meetings.

*Meetings of the entire child care center staff are held on the second and fourth Tuesday of each month. Attendance at staff meetings is mandatory, and the contribution of ideas and concerns from each individual is valued.*

Thank you for your cooperation in this matter.

# POLICY MEMORANDUM #10: UPCOMING TEACHER INSERVICE

To:     Child Care Center Staff

From: Child Care Center Director

Re:     Upcoming Teacher Inservice

Date: _____

On _____ from _____ until _____, _____ will provide a workshop for Center staff on _____. Dr./Mr./Ms. _____ is _____ and brings many years of experience with children to this training. Attendance at this workshop is mandatory for teaching staff. We have requested parent volunteers to help monitor the children during nap time.

Thank you for your cooperation in this matter.

# POLICY MEMORANDUM #11: MAINSTREAMED CHILDREN

**Child Care Center**

To:     Child Care Center Staff

From: Child Care Center Director

Re:     Mainstreamed Children

Date: ———————————————

According to federal law, we are pleased to welcome families rearing children with special needs to our program. The law requires programs receiving federal funds to accept a percentage of children with special needs. Accordingly, some of our children have been identified by specialists as having speech, hearing, behavioral, or other special needs. Please be assured that staff will receive all information necessary to support the development of all children participating. Our program is ideal for addressing special needs, as research indicates that when delays are remedied in early childhood, there is often less need for special education in elementary or secondary school.

If you or parents of our children have any questions about the mainstreaming process, please discuss these with me. Thank you for your efforts to provide quality care and education for young children.

# POLICY MEMORANDUM #12: FIELD TRIPS

## Child Care Center

To:     Child Care Center Staff

From: Child Care Center Director

Re:     Field Trips

Date: _____

This serves as a reminder of Center policies concerning field trips scheduled with Center children. Policy is further outlined in the *Staff Handbook*.

*Staff are welcome to share their ideas for field trips with the Center Director. All trips, whether walking or transported by bus, must be approved by the Center Director. Teachers should present trip ideas along with a suggested date and costs of the trip at least two weeks prior to the suggested date. Permission for child participation in trips must be secured from parents using the Center's Trip Permission Forms. In no instance will a child be permitted to participate in a trip unless a signed permission slip has been received at the Center.*

*Field trips are expected to be developmentally-appropriate settings, preferably related to themes under discussion in the classroom.*

*Teachers taking children on field trips must take along a list of children's allergies, medications, and emergency contact numbers. A first-aid kit, tissue for noses, bottled water, a cell phone, and one extra roll of toilet tissue should also be carried by teachers on field trips. Lunch and/or snack foods as may be needed for the outing should accompany teachers on field trips, and each child should wear a tag identifying the Center name, address, and telephone. Children should not wear name tags.*

# POLICY MEMORANDUM #13: ACCIDENT REPORTS

## Child Care Center

To:     Child Care Center Staff

From:  Child Care Center Director

Re:     Accident Reports

Date: _____

A reminder that at any time a child or staff member or visitor to the Center is injured on the premises or while on a class walk or field trip, a witnessing member of the staff must complete an Accident Report Form and file it in the main office within 24 hours of the incident. Accident Report Forms are available in the main office.

Accident Report Forms offer a documented method of describing the cause and nature of an accident as well as the method of treatment administered. They provide a record that may be requested by a physician, parents, or legal authorities

FIGURE 3.3

# ACCIDENT REPORT FORM

Name of injured person: _____

Date of accident: _____

Location of accident: _____

Description of accident: _____

_____

_____

_____

_____

_____

_____

_____

Response to accident/treatment of injury: _____

_____

_____

_____

_____

_____

Accident treated by: _____

Accident reported to: _____ Date/time: _____

Staff witnessing accident: _____ Date: _____

# POLICY MEMORANDUM #14:
# USE OF CENTER TELEPHONES

To:     Child Care Center Staff

From: Child Care Center Director

Re:     Use of Center Telephones

Date: _____

    Staff are reminded that Center telephones are for emergency use only, and may not be used for casual conversations. All personal telephone conversations by staff should be kept to a minimum length. Messages will be taken for any incoming personal telephone calls for staff members, except those that are designated as emergency in nature. Parents needing to use a telephone should be directed to the main office.

# POLICY MEMORANDUM #15: STANDARDIZED TESTING

**Child Care Center**

To:     Child Care Center Staff

From:   Child Care Center Director

Re:     Standardized Testing

Date:   _____

    Beginning on _____, teachers will be conducting the _____, a standardized test designed to assess children's levels of development. This test and procedures for administering the test will be thoroughly explained by a representative of the company that publishes the test.

    Tests can be a cause of great anxiety for all. This is not a paper-and-pencil test. Teachers will conduct activities much like those that usually go on in the classroom, observe the children, and record the results on forms provided. After all children have been tested, the results will be tallied by computer and will be available for parents and teachers.

    As parents are notified about the testing period, they may have questions. Any questions may be referred to the Center Director. Parents can be reassured by staff that these tests do not measure intelligence or aptitude, and no grouping will result from testing. Parent–teacher conferences will be scheduled after results have been compiled. All test results will be confidential.

    Please stop at the main office to discuss any additional questions.

# POLICY MEMORANDUM #16: OBSERVATIONS OF CHILDREN

**Child Care Center**

To:     Child Care Center Staff

From: Child Care Center Director

Re:     Observations of Children

Date: _____

Observations are one of the key methods for gathering information about children at the Center. Teaching staff are encouraged to conduct at least one informal observation of each child in their classrooms each week, and one formal observation, with a written record, each month. Sample observation forms are available in the main office and variations in recording styles will be discussed at an upcoming staff meeting. Written records of child observations are to be kept in a secure location where parents, volunteers, and other visitors to the Center do not have access.

Thank you for your cooperation and discretion regarding child and family privacy.

FIGURE 3.4

# OBSERVATION OF PSYCHOSOCIAL DEVELOPMENT: INFANT LEVEL

Child's name: _____ Date of birth: _____

Observation time: _____ to _____

Other adults present during the observation: _____

Location of observation: _____

1. Describe the activities of the child during your observation (e.g., eating, playing, toileting/changing, etc.). _____

_____

_____

2. Select one adult who seems to interact most with the child. Describe the ways that adult interacts with the child, such as talking to, picking up or holding, etc. _____

_____

_____

3. Describe how the child responds to overtures from the adult, such as by holding up arms to be picked up, by cuddling, or by pulling away.

_____

_____

4. If distressed or tired, does the child seek out the adult? Describe how the child seeks attention and how the adult responds. _____

_____

_____

5. Does the child seek assistance with materials or equipment from the adult? Describe. _____

_____

_____

6. Does the child interact with other children during the observation? If so, describe the nature of the interaction; e.g., playing quietly, sharing toys, quarreling, etc. _____

_____

_____

FIGURE 3.5

# OBSERVATION OF COGNITIVE DEVELOPMENT: TODDLER LEVEL

Child's name: _____ Date of birth: _____

Observation time: _____ to _____

Other adults present during the observation: _____

Location of observation: _____

1. Describe the activities and materials that the child is involved in during the observation, such as playing with blocks or a doll, eating, etc.

_____

_____

2. Describe the ways that the child handles any materials he/she encounters (e.g., mouthing, squeezing, smelling, staring at, rubbing).

_____

_____

3. Does the child appear to experiment with the materials encountered? Describe.

_____

_____

4. Does the child vocalize, ask questions, or show the materials to an adult? Describe.

_____

_____

5. What language or vocalization does the child engage in while playing?

_____

_____

6. What concepts (ideas or knowledge) does the child appear to have? How do you know?

_____

_____

7. At what level of cognitive development, according to Piaget, would you place this child?

_____

_____

FIGURE 3.6

# OBSERVATION OF PHYSICAL DEVELOPMENT: PRESCHOOL LEVEL

Child's name: _____ Date of birth: _____

Observation time: _____ to _____

Other adults present during the observation: _____

Location of observation: _____

1. Describe the activities that you observe the child engaged in. _____

_____

_____

2. Describe the gross motor abilities of the child. _____

_____

_____

3. Describe the fine motor abilities of the child. _____

_____

_____

4. Does the child seek help from an adult in order to complete age-appropriate activities? Describe. _____

_____

_____

5. Does the child appear to have age-appropriate physical skills? Describe._____

_____

_____

6. What physical activities do you prescribe and why? _____

_____

_____

# POLICY MEMORANDUM #17: BULLETIN BOARDS/ CLASSROOM DISPLAYS

To:     Child Care Center Staff

From:  Child Care Center Director

Re:     Bulletin Boards/Classroom Displays

Date: _____

Teachers are encouraged to make regular use of bulletin boards and other classroom displays. As bulletin boards are not at the children's eye level, they are best used to educate and inform parents. Although seasonal or holiday displays are colorful, the boards are better used when informing parents about the curriculum and the children's activities.

Bulletin boards should not be used to display children's work. Children's art and other projects should be displayed where they can see them, on walls or tables at children's eye levels.

In no case should bulletin boards or other displays be left in place for more than two weeks. These areas are to be used for education and information and should be changed regularly.

Thank you for your cooperation in this matter.

# POLICY MEMORANDUM #18: CLASSROOM CLEANLINESS

To:     Child Care Center Staff

From:   Child Care Center Director

Re:     Classroom Cleanliness

Date:   _____

Teachers are required to leave all classrooms in order at the end of each day. After wiping table tops, chairs should be placed on top, all toys and books should be shelved, and cots should be stacked. These efforts assure that the Center's maintenance engineer can sweep and mop floors. Trash and other items to be discarded should be placed inside of classrooms and near classroom doors. Please use the containers provided for recyclable materials.

If significant spills or accidents occur during the school day, teachers should notify the maintenance engineer immediately to avoid slips and falls.

# POLICY MEMORANDUM #19: EMERGENCY EVACUATION PLAN

**Child Care Center**

To:      Child Care Center Staff

From:  Child Care Center Director

Re:      Emergency Evacuation Plan

Date:  _____

    In the event of fire, inclement weather, or other emergency requiring evacuation from the Center, teachers and other staff should follow the Emergency Evacuation Plan posted in each classroom. At the sound of the fire alarm or upon direction from an administrator, the Plan directs staff to:

1. Notify police, fire department, or other emergency personnel of the evacuation.
2. Gather children's emergency contact information and the Center cell phone.
3. Lead children quickly and calmly to the nearest exit from the building.
4. Once outside, all children and teachers should gather at

    _____.

5. Begin contacting children's emergency contacts to arrange pick-ups.

© 2002 by The Center for Applied Research in Education

# POLICY MEMORANDUM #20: WORKING WITH VOLUNTEERS

**Child Care Center**

To:     Child Care Center Staff

From:  Child Care Center Director

Re:     Working with Volunteers

Date: _____

Parents are always welcome to visit the Center and volunteer in their children's classrooms. Students completing student teaching and/or practicum experiences and community members will also be volunteering their time at the Center. Our volunteers are very important to us, making it possible for children to receive more one-on-one attention, and for staff to conduct additional small-group activities.

However, volunteers must be oriented by the Director before beginning work in classrooms. Only parents may work in the classroom without submission of criminal history, child abuse, and health clearances, as these are not required by law.

A volunteer is expected to sign in at the main office on arrival, check in with teachers in the classroom where he/she will work, and then be given a work assignment by the lead teacher. Volunteers should expect to receive thoughtful and supportive feedback from staff. If a volunteer creates a problem or a disturbance in the classroom, this problem should be referred to the Center Director.

# POLICY MEMORANDUM # 21: HOME–SCHOOL MEETINGS

To:     Child Care Center Staff

From: Child Care Center Director

Re:     Home–School Meetings

Date: _____

Home–School Meetings are held monthly at the Center for parent information and education. Staff are required to attend these meetings on a rotating basis, approximately one meeting every four months.

A calendar of meetings and staff scheduled to attend is posted in the main office. When a staff member is scheduled to attend a Home–School Meeting, he/she is expected to meet that obligation except in emergency situations. If unable to attend a meeting, the staff member is expected to inform the Center Director and to make arrangements for another member of the staff to substitute at that meeting.

Thank you for your cooperation in this matter.

# POLICY MEMORANDUM #22: PARENT–TEACHER CONFERENCES

**Child Care Center**

To:     Child Care Center Staff

From:   Child Care Center Director

Re:     Parent–Teacher Conferences

Date:   _____

    Parent–teacher conferences are scheduled for the weeks of _____ and _____. Conferences will be held in the main office, the Staff Room, and in the Social Worker's office. The children's program is expected to continue during the time of the conferences. However, lead teachers will free themselves to meet with parents for one-half-hour conferences in the morning between _____ and _____, and in the afternoon between _____ and _____. Conferences will also be held during the evening of _____ between _____ and _____. Lead teachers should be available on this evening and will receive compensatory time for hours worked. Additional staff will be asked to provide child care services during the evening conference hours.

    In preparation for the conferences, teachers should begin reviewing and updating children's folders. A parent–teacher conference sign-up sheet accompanies this memo and should be placed in a prominent location in each classroom. Parents have been notified by letter of the procedures for scheduling a conference.

    Following each conference, teachers are asked to record the results of the conference on the forms provided by the Center.

FIGURE 3.7

# PARENT–TEACHER CONFERENCE
# SIGN-UP SHEET

Classroom ——————— Teacher —————————————————

| Date | Time | Parent's Name |
|------|------|---------------|
|  |  |  |
|  |  |  |
|  |  |  |
|  |  |  |
|  |  |  |
|  |  |  |
|  |  |  |
|  |  |  |
|  |  |  |
|  |  |  |
|  |  |  |
|  |  |  |
|  |  |  |
|  |  |  |
|  |  |  |
|  |  |  |

FIGURE 3.8

# PARENT–TEACHER CONFERENCE RECORD

Classroom _____ Teacher _____

Parent's name _____ Child's name _____

Date of conference _____ Time of conference _____

Records reviewed _____

_____

_____

Issues discussed _____

_____

_____

_____

_____

_____

Goals set for child _____

_____

_____

_____

_____

Teacher's Signature _____ Date _____

# POLICY MEMORANDUM #23:
# HOME VISITS

**Child Care Center**

To:     Child Care Center Staff

From: Child Care Center Director

Re:     Home Visits

Date: _____

   Parents will soon be notified that home visits will be conducted during the week of _____. Home visits will be conducted by teachers traveling in teams of two. The Center will be closed for children's programming during the week of home visiting.

   During children's nap times, please use the attached form and begin contacting parents by telephone to request a home visit. Home visits are voluntary on the part of families, and no parents should be criticized for refusing a visit. The visits should be explained as a way of further getting to know children and their families. Many children behave differently, more comfortably in their own homes. It is not a time for conducting a written observation of families. Techniques for home visits will be discussed at the upcoming staff meeting.

   If you or parents have questions regarding the nature or purpose of home visits, I will be pleased to answer these individually or during our next staff meeting.

FIGURE 3.9

# HOME-VISITS SCHEDULING FORM

Classroom ———————— Teacher ——————————————————

| Date | Time | Parent | Address/Telephone |
|------|------|--------|-------------------|
| ———— | ———— | ———————————— | ———————————— |
| ———— | ———— | ———————————— | ———————————— |
| ———— | ———— | ———————————— | ———————————— |
| ———— | ———— | ———————————— | ———————————— |
| ———— | ———— | ———————————— | ———————————— |
| ———— | ———— | ———————————— | ———————————— |
| ———— | ———— | ———————————— | ———————————— |
| ———— | ———— | ———————————— | ———————————— |
| ———— | ———— | ———————————— | ———————————— |
| ———— | ———— | ———————————— | ———————————— |
| ———— | ———— | ———————————— | ———————————— |
| ———— | ———— | ———————————— | ———————————— |
| ———— | ———— | ———————————— | ———————————— |
| ———— | ———— | ———————————— | ———————————— |
| ———— | ———— | ———————————— | ———————————— |
| ———— | ———— | ———————————— | ———————————— |
| ———— | ———— | ———————————— | ———————————— |
| ———— | ———— | ———————————— | ———————————— |
| ———— | ———— | ———————————— | ———————————— |

FIGURE 3.10

# RECORD OF HOME VISIT

Classroom _____ Teacher _____

Parent's name _____ Child's name _____

Date of home visit _____ Time of visit _____

Home address_____ Telephone _____

Issues discussed _____

_____

_____

_____

_____

_____

_____

_____

Goals set for child _____

_____

_____

_____

_____

_____

_____

_____

Teacher's Signature _____ Date _____

# POLICY MEMORANDUM #24: DAILY SCHEDULE FOR CHILDREN

To:      Child Care Center Staff

From:  Child Care Center Director

Re:      Daily Schedule for Children

Date: _____

Teachers in each classroom may set their own daily schedules for children. However, schedules should be appropriate to children's needs and flexible to allow for day-to-day events. A daily schedule should be posted in each classroom. The following should be included in each schedule:

- a balance of active and quiet times
- both small- and large-group activities
- regular toileting and wash-up times
- outdoor and indoor play
- two snacks and lunch periods
- a nap time of 60 to 90 minutes
- both free-choice times and organized activities

Thank you for your cooperation and support of developmentally-appropriate practices.

# POLICY MEMORANDUM #25: DEVELOPMENTALLY-APPROPRIATE CURRICULUM

To:     Child Care Center Staff

From:   Child Care Center Director

Re:     Developmentally-Appropriate Curriculum

Date: _____

Our Center is dedicated to the application of curriculum that is developmentally-appropriate to the needs of the children we serve. For this reason, teachers will avoid the use of ditto (reproducible) sheets, forced writing, reading, or calculation activities, or daily homework. Through our inservice and other teacher-education activities, we strive to inform teachers about the reasons for an early childhood approach to the education of young children. However, we recognize that parents may feel pressure, and in turn apply that pressure to teachers, to use "push-down" curriculum designed for the elementary school.

At the time of enrollment, parents are fully informed of the type of program offered at the Center. Furthermore, explanations of the nature of the curriculum are provided in the *Parents' Handbook*. If, at any time, teachers or other staff feel unable to answer parents' questions about the rationale for our children's programming, please refer those parents to the Center Director for further information.

# POLICY MEMORANDUM #26: HANDLING OF CHILDREN'S SNACKS AND MEALTIMES

To:    Child Care Center Staff

From: Child Care Center Director

Re:    Handling of Children's Snacks and Mealtimes

Date: _____

    Please be advised that children's snacks and meals are to be served family style. Children, except in the infant and toddler groups, are to serve themselves from serving dishes with adult supervision.

    Furthermore, an adult is to be seated with children at each table. This is designed to reduce mealtime tension and promote children's socialization.

    Thank you for your cooperation in this matter.

# POLICY MEMORANDUM #27:
# INDIVIDUAL IN CHARGE
# DURING DIRECTOR'S ABSENCE

Child Care Center

To:     Child Care Center Staff

From:  Child Care Center Director

Re:     Individual in Charge During Director's Absence

Date: _____

There have recently been some questions as to lines of authority during the absence of the Center Director. When the Director is not on the premises, due to illness, vacation, meetings or other obligations, _____ will assume the director's duties. In the event that both the Director and _____ are absent from the Center, then the lead teacher in the preschool classroom will be responsible for the Center. This means that decisions are to be made, deliveries received, and other directorial duties will be performed by these individuals.

Thank you for your cooperation in this matter and support of our program.

# POLICY MEMORANDUM #28: ORDERING OF CLASSROOM SUPPLIES

To:     Child Care Center Staff

From:  Child Care Center Director

Re:     Ordering of Classroom Supplies

Date: _____

Supplies for individual classrooms may be requested by classroom lead teachers at any time during the school year. Staff will be advised when their supply allocation has been exhausted.

When requesting supplies, it is recommended that teachers consider the following criteria. The Director reserves the right to deny any supply requests that do not meet this criteria.

- developmental appropriateness
- safety
- durability
- attractiveness to children
- multiple uses
- cost (portion of budget allocation)
- match with classroom themes
- sustained interest to children
- use by multiple children
- storage needs

Thank you for your cooperation in this matter and support of our program.

# POLICY MEMORANDUM #29: STAFF OBSERVATIONS AND EVALUATIONS

Child Care Center

To:     Child Care Center Staff

From: Child Care Center Director

Re:     Staff Observations and Evaluations

Date: _____

As described in the *Staff Handbook,* staff evaluations are conducted annually. These consist of Director observations of classroom teachers and written evaluations and conferences with all staff members. Observations of classroom teachers will be conducted during the week of _____.

No advance notice will be given of observation days and times. Each observation will last approximately one hour. At the conclusion of all teacher observations, the Director will distribute all staff evaluations and begin scheduling of conferences. In the event of staff absence during the observation week, an observation will be conducted the following week.

Staff are counseled that evaluations are confidential and should not be discussed or compared, as each staff member has different strengths and needs for development.

Thank you for your cooperation in this matter.

FIGURE 3.11

# CHILD CARE CENTER CLASSROOM STAFF OBSERVATION

Name _____ Position _____

Observer _____ Date/time of observation _____

Types of activities observed _____

_____

_____

_____

_____

Role observed in activities _____

_____

_____

_____

_____

Quality of interaction with children _____

_____

_____

_____

Quality of interaction with co-workers _____

_____

_____

_____

_____

Quality of interaction with parents/volunteers _____

_____

_____

_____

_____

Overall rating of performance _____

_____

_____

_____

FIGURE 3.12

# CHILD CARE CENTER STAFF EVALUATION

Name _____ Position _____

Length of employment _____ Date of evaluation _____

| | Frequently | Rarely | Never |
|---|---|---|---|
| **I. Professionalism** | | | |
| A. Reports to work on time. | _____ | _____ | _____ |
| B. Reports unexpected lateness. | _____ | _____ | _____ |
| C. Gives advance notice of vacation requests. | _____ | _____ | _____ |
| D. Dresses according to Center policy. | _____ | _____ | _____ |
| E. Represents Center effectively with visitors. | _____ | _____ | _____ |
| F. Relates positively to co-workers. | _____ | _____ | _____ |
| G. Supports professional activity of co-workers. | _____ | _____ | _____ |
| H. Reports problems to supervisors. | _____ | _____ | _____ |
| I. Works to resolve issues with co-workers. | _____ | _____ | _____ |
| J. Seeks professional-growth activities. | _____ | _____ | _____ |
| K. Demonstrates a positive work attitude. | _____ | _____ | _____ |
| L. Goes beyond parameters of job description. | _____ | _____ | _____ |
| M. Observes confidentiality | _____ | _____ | _____ |

Comments _____

_____

_____

_____

| | Frequently | Rarely | Never |
|---|---|---|---|
| **II. Interactions with Children** | | | |
| A. Shows enjoyment/appreciation of children. | _____ | _____ | _____ |
| B. Uses a respectful, pleasant tone with children. | _____ | _____ | _____ |
| C. Stoops or sits at children's eye level. | _____ | _____ | _____ |
| D. Demonstrates knowledge of children's developmental levels. | _____ | _____ | _____ |
| E. Treats children as individual/unique. | _____ | _____ | _____ |
| F. Implements individual activities with children. | _____ | _____ | _____ |
| G. Implements small-group activities with children. | _____ | _____ | _____ |
| H. Implements whole-group activities with children. | _____ | _____ | _____ |
| I. Demonstrates ability to assess individual needs. | _____ | _____ | _____ |
| J. Plans for individual needs. | _____ | _____ | _____ |
| K. Assists in planning overall curriculum. | _____ | _____ | _____ |
| L. Assists in selecting materials/equipment. | _____ | _____ | _____ |
| M. Maintains records on children's progress. | _____ | _____ | _____ |

FIGURE 3.12 (*continued*)

N. Promotes physical development. _____ _____ _____
O. Promotes cognitive development. _____ _____ _____
P. Promotes psychosocial development. _____ _____ _____

Comments _____

_____

_____

| III. Interactions with Families | Frequently | Rarely | Never |
|---|---|---|---|
| A. Treats parents/caretakers with respect. | _____ | _____ | _____ |
| B. Supports families' goals for their children. | _____ | _____ | _____ |
| C. Treats parents/caretakers as individuals. | _____ | _____ | _____ |
| D. Respects cultures and customs of families. | _____ | _____ | _____ |
| E. Listens to parent/caretaker concerns. | _____ | _____ | _____ |
| F. Communicates regularly with parents about children's progress. | _____ | _____ | _____ |
| G. Communicates in a professional yet accessible manner. | _____ | _____ | _____ |
| H. Follows up after meeting with parents. | _____ | _____ | _____ |
| I. Observes family privacy and confidences. | _____ | _____ | _____ |
| J. Seeks parent/caretaker input. | _____ | _____ | _____ |
| K. Successfully involves parents/caretakers in program. | _____ | _____ | _____ |
| L. Welcomes parents/caretakers into classroom. | _____ | _____ | _____ |
| M. Reports parent concerns to supervisor. | _____ | _____ | _____ |

Comments _____

_____

_____

**IV. Overall Rating (circle one)**

Excellent          Very Good          Making Progress          Poor

Staff comments _____

_____

_____

_____     _____     _____
Evaluator Signature              Title                    Date

_____     _____     _____
Staff Signature                  Title                    Date

# POLICY MEMORANDUM #30: STAFF BREAK TIMES

**Child Care Center**

To:      Child Care Center Staff

From:  Child Care Center Director

Re:      Staff Break Times

Date: _____

According to state employment laws and Center policies (see *Staff Handbook*), staff are entitled to _____ breaks during each work day. Staff are not only entitled to breaks, but are encouraged to take them away from the children. However, some have been observed taking longer breaks that infringe on the free time of others.

When taking a break, teaching staff should assure that there is adequate coverage in the classroom and then inform and/or request that they would like to use their break time. Volunteers may never be left alone with children. Non-teaching staff should advise the Center Director or other administrator when planning to take a break. At no time should staff leave for a break without advising another staff member. Staff should then return promptly to the classroom or other duty when the break period is over.

Observation of break-time rules makes the atmosphere more comfortable for all staff. Thank you for your cooperation in this matter.

# POLICY MEMORANDUM #31: CHANGE IN STAFF INSURANCE COVERAGE

To:     Child Care Center Staff

From: Child Care Center Director

Re:     Change in Staff Insurance Coverage

Date: _____

As you are aware, the Center's Advisory Board has been meeting to determine a means to add dental insurance to the staff benefits package. I am pleased to announce that as of _____, staff will be able to add dental coverage provided by _____.

Parameters of the new dental coverage will be discussed at the next staff meeting. At that time you will receive enrollment forms and written material on the policy. As you may have many questions about the new coverage, we hope to have an insurance company representative present at the meeting.

# POLICY MEMORANDUM #32: PLAYGROUND SUPERVISION

To:     Child Care Center Staff

From: Child Care Center Director

Re:     Playground Supervision

Date: _____

As a result of my observations, it has come to my attention that children may be inadequately supervised while on the playground. Since outdoor play is an important part of children's development, staff should not congregate to talk while children are running about or using the outdoor equipment. Staff should be stationed around the play yard where they can clearly observe children's activities.

I welcome any suggestions for improvement of playground supervision. If we are to be effective in preventing outdoor accidents and maximize children's use of outdoor play time, we must be supervising and facilitating that play.

© 2002 by The Center for Applied Research in Education

# "BACK TO SLEEP" REMINDER

To:     Child Care Center Staff

From:   Child Care Center Director

Re:     "Back to Sleep" Reminder

Date: _____

The American Academy of Pediatrics and other children's health organizations are actively promoting the "Back to Sleep" campaign. This promotion urges parents and other caregivers to put babies to sleep on their backs, as this has been found to reduce the instance of Sudden Infant Death Syndrome (SIDS or crib death) by 40% worldwide. Although the correlation between stomach sleeping and SIDS is unclear, we know that back sleeping is a deterrent to tragedy. *All infants at the Center must be put to sleep on their backs.*

You may have heard that motor delays have been attributed to back sleeping. Some babies have been found to be slower to push up, sit up, and crawl, and this has been tied to spending less crib time on their stomachs. Researchers have also found that giving babies adequate floor time for play during the day compensates for lack of play time in the crib. *All babies at the Center should have at least one-half hour of supervised play time on the floor twice each day.*

# CONDOLENCE

Dear _____:

All of your co-workers, children, and parents at the Center were saddened to learn of the death of _____. We realize that you had a very special relationship with _____ and can only imagine how great your loss must be.

Please think of us as your extended family, and call upon us to assist you in any way. Some of the staff will receive release time to attend the services for your _____ on _____. Please know that we are all with you in spirit.

Sincerely,

_____

Center Director

# ENCOURAGEMENT AT A DIFFICULT TIME

## Child Care Center

Dear _____:

I wanted you to know that I have watched your struggle as you have continued your education at the college, worked at the Center, and tried to take care of your family. As you have neared the end of your degree program, you have seemed increasingly tired and sometimes discouraged.

All of your colleagues are behind you in your efforts to grow personally and professionally, and believe me when I say that although it may seem overwhelming now, it will be worth all the investment that you have made.

Please let us, your colleagues and friends, know if we can be of additional support.

Sincerely,


_____

Center Director

# CONGRATULATIONS FOR DEGREE EARNED

Dear _____:

    You have done it! Congratulations on receipt of your _____ Degree in Early Childhood Education! This is an enormous achievement for you, for your family that supported your efforts, and for all of us, your co-workers, at the Center. We are all so very proud of you!

    Your diligence in pursuit of higher education, the long hours of study, and the commitment that you demonstrate daily to the children are all a part of your strong character. These and other traits make you an invaluable member of our staff.

    Our very best wishes to you and your family on this marvelous occasion.

Sincerely,

_____

Center Director

# COPING WITH PROBLEMS: CONFLICT WITH A FAMILY

Dear _____:

   I am aware of the disagreement that has arisen between you and _____. I appreciate the time and concern you have given to a resolution to this situation. I will be meeting with this parent on _____ at _____, and request that you join us at that time. Please bring with you any notes you may have made to document this problem.

   I am hopeful that there will be a positive resolution of this situation. Thank you for your cooperation in this matter.

Sincerely,


_____
Center Director

# COPING WITH PROBLEMS: CHRONIC LATENESS

Child Care Center

Dear _____:

I have noticed over a period of several weeks a pattern of lateness developing around your arrival at the Center. I know that we discussed changes that have occurred in your personal situation, but I had hoped that the matter would be resolved by now. Perhaps another staff member or a parent will have information that will help to resolve this dilemma. I am also available to meet with you to assist you in resolving this situation.

As per Center policy (see the *Staff Handbook*), I must deduct the time missed from the paycheck that you will receive next week. The children, the parents, and the other staff count on you to be there at the start of each day. I continue to believe that this problem will be resolved in the immediate future.

Sincerely,

_____

Center Director

# COPING WITH PROBLEMS: CONFLICT BETWEEN STAFF

**Child Care Center**

Dear _____:

    Thank you for coming to see me regarding the disagreement with _____. I know that the problems between you must be very troubling, as you have always been cooperative co-workers. I sometimes think that the work we do with children and families can be very stressful, and this can tax even strong friendships.

    I know that you are aware that we must resolve any dissension quickly as it impacts on both of you, on children, and on other staff. I am asking that you and _____ meet with me in my office on _____ during the children's nap time. Our meeting will be confidential, and no one else need know the nature of it. The purpose of our talk is to try to resolve the differences between you. You are both very dedicated, and I am certain that we can find a solution to the current problem.

    Thank you for seeking support in coping with this issue.

Sincerely,

_____

Center Director

# COPING WITH PROBLEMS: CHILD-ABUSE ALLEGATION

Child Care Center

Dear _____:

I know that you are aware that a parent, _____, has complained that during _____ in _____ you _____ her child, _____. I can only imagine how distressed you must be. As per Center policy, I will be meeting with this child's parents to discuss the matter, and will also meet privately with you to try to get a more clear picture of the events of that day.

The parent has agreed not to notify Child Protective Services until we have talked, as she understands the profound impact of an allegation of this type on your career in child care. Prior to our meeting, please review your thoughts on that day's activities, and put into writing a clear description of your recollections.

I appreciate your cooperation in this matter, and will attempt to clarify the circumstances of this situation as soon as possible.

Sincerely,

_____
Center Director

© 2002 by The Center for Applied Research in Education

# COPING WITH PROBLEMS: WORK SUSPENSION

Dear _____ :

I regret to inform you of your indefinite suspension without pay from the child care center, effective immediately.

Since meeting with _____ regarding her allegations that you _____ her child, several of your co-workers have come forward to say that they witnessed the incident. Unfortunately, they have stated in writing that _____. The parent has informed us that she is filing a child-abuse complaint with Child Protective Services, and this child is being removed from the Center. Pending an investigation by the state, you will be suspended from your position as a teacher's aide at the Center.

Please contact me at _____ if you have questions regarding this decision, or your rights as described in the *Staff Handbook*.

Sincerely,


_____
Center Director

# COPING WITH PROBLEMS: WARNING REGARDING STAFF INAPPROPRIATE BEHAVIOR

Dear _____:

   Several staff members have approached me to complain that you have used inappropriate sexual language and innuendo in their presence. As I have not witnessed this behavior, I do not know the actual circumstances or your behavior. I would like to take this opportunity, however, to remind you that the child care center has strict policies about what may be considered sexual harassment.

   This letter serves as an official warning that all staff, males and females, must refrain from making comments about real or proposed sexual activity, private body parts, or other personal matters in the presence of colleagues who may find such discussion offensive. A federal law protects workers from just such intimidation at their job sites.

   I know that you are aware that a comfortable and supportive work environment is essential to the well-being of staff and the effectiveness of our program. Please feel free to discuss this matter with me personally if you have any questions.

   Thank you for your cooperation.

Sincerely,


_____
Center Director

© 2002 by The Center for Applied Research in Education

# COPING WITH PROBLEMS: DISMISSAL OF A STAFF MEMBER

Child Care Center

Dear _____:

Although you have received several letters of warning, and we have met on three different occasions to discuss this issue, your inappropriate behavior toward female staff at our Center has persisted. This cannot be tolerated. Staff must feel that they are in a safe and comfortable work environment. As you know, several of your colleagues have made written complaints regarding your conduct, and their accusations, the witnesses to this behavior, and my assessment of this situation reinforce my decision that the Center is no longer the appropriate place for your employment.

Therefore, your position as _____ is hereby terminated, effective immediately. Be advised that because of the nature of your dismissal, I will be unable to give a reference for any future employment that you might seek. Your final paycheck will be mailed to the home address on file.

Sincerely,


_____

Center Director

# WORKER'S COMPENSATION CLAIM

Dear ——————————:

    I am in receipt of your letter of ——————— concerning your back injury and the supporting documentation from your physician. As described in the *Staff Handbook*, we do indeed provide Worker's Compensation Insurance. I understand that your injury may be serious enough to require that you receive full short-term disability insurance. However, I do not make that determination.

    In order to make and process a claim for disability, please contact the state Worker's Compensation Claims Information Helpline at 1-800-555-5555. They will assist in processing your claim, and will forward paperwork to me for my input and signature.

    You are missed by the children and staff, and we hope that you will be feeling better and back with us soon.

Sincerely,


———————————————
Center Director

© 2002 by The Center for Applied Research in Education

# TUITION ASSISTANCE PLAN

## Child Care Center

Dear _____ :

Congratulations on your success at college! We are all proud of your efforts to learn more about the profession and appreciative of the way that you have shared information with us.

In accordance with the newly acted Tuition Assistance Plan, you must submit a copy of your final grade report, paid tuition bill, and bill for books, and the Center will reimburse one-half of these costs. As long as you have achieved a grade of "C" or better in your courses, we will reimburse you for the agreed-upon share. Please continue your schooling as it benefits not only you, but our entire Program!

Best wishes.

Sincerely,

_____

Center Director

# APPRECIATION
# FOR A JOB WELL DONE

Dear ———————————:

    I certainly did not anticipate the ——————— while I was away at the National Association for the Education of Young Children Conference last week. It was knowing that I could count on your professionalism in my absence that made it possible for me to attend without anxiety. With the onset of ———————, you made all the right decisions: contacting ———————, the Policy Board Chair, regarding an emergency closing; assigning staff to begin contacting parents; and staying yourself at the Center until the last child had been picked up. As a result, Center functioning was smooth and effective.

    As always, you demonstrated outstanding leadership skills that went beyond your role as head teacher. In a few years, I am certain that you will be putting those abilities to even better use as the director of a child care program.

    Thank you for a job well done!

Sincerely,


—————————————————

Center Director

# REFERENCE

## Child Care Center

Dear _____:

It is with great pleasure that I write to recommend _____ for the _____ position at _____. _____ has been with our Program for _____ years, during which time she earned her _____ Degree in early childhood education.

_____ has been an enthusiastic and competent staff member from the first. She began as a teacher's aide and, after receipt of her degree, competed for the position of classroom teacher. _____ is creative and energetic in her interactions with children, supportive and concerned with co-workers and parents. She has always gone beyond the parameters of her job descriptions, assuming many additional responsibilities.

I have no doubt that _____ will be an exceptional _____ in your program, and an invaluable member of your staff. Please contact me at _____ if additional information is required.

Sincerely,

_____

Center Director

# AS YOU MOVE ON

## Child Care Center

Dear _____:

    Congratulations on your new position as _____ at _____! It is an overdue and well-deserved move. In many senses, however, your gain is our loss. You have been a strong and positive influence among the staff, always willing to go above and beyond what was required.

    I have observed your growth with pride and a conviction that you were destined for success. As you move on to your new role, remember us, and keep in touch to let us know about subsequent changes in your life.

    Best wishes from Center children, families, and staff for a bright and happy future.

Sincerely,


_____

Center Director

# AS YOU RETIRE

Child Care Center

Dear _____:

The occasion of your retirement is both a joyful and sad time. You have brightened the lives and influenced the development of countless children and families in your many years as an early childhood educator. Our Center will simply not be the same without you!

Still there comes time to move on to a new phase of life, to new challenges and experiences. We know that you will soon be exploring new activities and friendships, but hope that you will not forget those who love you at our Center.

Our very best wishes to you as this new doorway opens wide.

Sincerely,

_____

Center Director

# AWARD ANNOUNCEMENT

Dear _____:

   I am pleased to present to you the _____ award for the month of _____. This is a small way to acknowledge your consistent and invaluable contribution to our Center. In particular I would like to recognize your skill(s) _____. Our work can be stressful and difficult, and it is the efforts of team members like yourself that make our work easier and more rewarding.

   On behalf of your colleagues, children, and families, thank you for putting your talents and energies to use at our Center.

Sincerely,


_____
Center Director

FIGURE 3.13

# TEACHER-OF-THE-MONTH
# CERTIFICATE

FIGURE 3.14

## STAFF-MEMBER-OF-THE-MONTH CERTIFICATE

Staff Member of the Month

Teacher

Director

# Letters to Board and Community Members

Many early childhood agencies are required by federal guidelines or by-laws to recruit a board of advisory community members. The board oversees the workings of the program and tenders advice when required. Advisory boards may be comprised of parents, community leaders, and others who have expertise to contribute. In some cases, child care center directors report directly to their boards, considered the final authority. While directors make day-to-day determinations, boards have input into any major decision-making.

The selection of advisory or policy board members is key. Administrators may solicit board participation from persons who reflect components of the program. A pediatrician can provide valuable input into center health, safety, and nutrition. An attorney can create simple contracts, permission forms, and other documents used in the program. Parents can provide insight into issues faced by clients and children. In all cases of invitations to board participation, solicitations should be made to persons who are capable of sound and objective thought, individuals who can put the best interests of the program ahead of personal needs.

In addition to the advisory board, early childhood leaders should look to the community around the center for additional avenues of involvement. A director's participation on the boards of other agencies can open doors to mutual support and projects. The community can be a rich source of volunteers to work with young children. Local businesses can be persuaded to "adopt" school and child care programs, endowing them with financial support, material donations, and in-kind services.

Another important element of the larger community is the schools young children enter upon kindergarten enrollment. A serious gap presently exists between many preschool centers and local feeder elementary schools. Kindergarten teachers know that many children have preschool experiences, but do not know precisely what those experiences consist of. These teachers may then have inappropriate expectations for new pupils. Furthermore, kindergarten entrance is a major passage for young children. This transition is eased when teachers in both programs communicate with one another, and visits are made between groups of children. Once children have moved on to elementary schools, their families become center alumni. These persons should continue as a part of the center "family," and kept apprised of program developments and events.

Sources of grants providing funds or materials also enrich early childhood programs. Administrators should be alert for foundations and government programs that address services to young children. Today these funding sources enable many agencies to expand and provide improved resources for families.

An early childhood program is not an island, but a vital and active component of an ever-changing community; a community rich in assets and expertise to be reaped on behalf of children and families.

# INVITATION TO JOIN CENTER'S ADVISORY BOARD

## Child Care Center

Dear ——————————————:

I was pleased to meet and talk with you at the Chamber of Commerce meeting on ——————.

Again, I would like to extend to you an invitation to become a member of our Center Advisory Board. Your unique expertise would be of great value to us in improving the services we offer to our children and their families. Our Board meets once each month on the third Tuesday at 7:00 P.M. Meetings are generally one and one-half hours long, and end promptly at 8:30 P.M.

In addition to the monthly Board meetings, there are several Center events each year that we urge Board members to participate in, including our annual Holiday Party for families.

Although your schedule is a busy one, I am certain that you will find involvement in our program rewarding. I have taken the liberty of enclosing the notice of our next Board meeting scheduled for —————————————. Please contact me at ——————— if I can answer any questions about our program or Board membership.

Thank you for your consideration in this matter.

Sincerely,

————————————————
Center Director

Enc.

# THANK-YOU FOR AGREEING TO JOIN BOARD

Dear _____:

On behalf of the Advisory Board, children, parents, and Center staff, we were delighted to receive your prompt acceptance of the offer of Board membership! I am certain that your contributions to our program will be invaluable, and that this experience will be as rewarding to you.

We look forward to seeing you at the Advisory Board meeting on _____.

Sincerely,

_____
Center Director

# NOTICE OF ADVISORY BOARD MEETING

Dear Board Member:

The next meeting of the _____ Advisory Board is scheduled for _____ at 7:00 P.M. in _____.

At that time the Board is slated to discuss the Program mission and goals for 2002–2003. Please advise the main office at _____ if you will be unable to attend. We look forward to your input.

Sincerely,


_____

Center Director

# REQUEST FOR ADVISORY BOARD FEEDBACK

Dear Advisory Board Member:

As you know, we recently applied for a grant from the Department of Health and Human Services to expand our program. A letter received in the main office on _____ indicated interest in our expansion plan but requested additional information about links to the community, including current résumés for members of our Advisory Board. The deadline for our response to this request is _____, and I will need this information from you no later than _____. Please contact me at _____ if you require further information about this request.

Thank you for your ongoing support of our program.

Sincerely,


_____

Center Director

© 2002 by The Center for Applied Research in Education

# RETIRING ADVISORY BOARD MEMBER

Dear _____:

On behalf of the entire Center family, thank you for your years of enthusiastic and dedicated service to our program! We will miss your commitment and the sense of direction that has helped to guide our endeavors. Supported by your input, our program has developed and expanded to serve many more children and parents.

As you move on to new projects, please think of us and keep us apprised of your activities. In turn, we will update you each month with a Center newsletter.

Our heart-felt thanks and best wishes.

Sincerely,


_____

Center Director

# CENTER DIRECTOR'S ACCEPTANCE OF COMMUNITY BOARD POSITION

Dear _____ :

    I was pleased to receive your letter of _____ regarding membership on the _____ Advisory Board and brochure describing your program. Your cause is one in which I have long had personal and professional interest.

    I am delighted to accept your invitation, and look forward to receiving information regarding the next Board meeting. I am enclosing a copy of my curriculum vitae for your records.

Sincerely,


_____
Center Director

Enc.

# CENTER DIRECTOR'S DECLINING COMMUNITY BOARD POSITION

Dear _____:

    I am in receipt of your kind letter of _____ inviting me to become a member of your agency's Advisory Board. I am aware of the fine work done by your program and the many years of service that you have provided to our community.

    Unfortunately, the many activities required of my current position prevent me from undertaking any additional projects at this time.

    I wish you continued success in your exceptional efforts to improve our community.

Sincerely,


_____

Center Director

# SOLICITING VOLUNTEERS

Dear _____:

It was a pleasure having the opportunity to talk with you about the work of our early childhood education program.

As you know, we are continually searching for volunteers to provide support for our teaching staff, and to provide additional one-on-one time to children. Volunteers work under the supervision of classroom teachers, and need no previous experience to be involved in our program. Volunteer activities include reading stories to children; helping with toileting, hand washing, and mealtime routines; assisting with activities set-up; and participation in walks and field trips. As required by state law for individuals working with children, volunteers must have criminal history, child abuse, and health clearances.

I would like to invite your employees to consider volunteering a few hours each week at our Center. While no pay is involved, the rewards that come from facilitating the development of a young child are limitless.

We will be holding a Volunteer Orientation Workshop on _____ at _____. If any staff from your firm are interested in attending this session, they should contact the Center at _____.

Thank you for your consideration in this matter.

Sincerely,


_____
Center Director

# REQUEST FOR VOLUNTEER INFORMATION

## Child Care Center

Dear _____:

We were delighted to meet you at the recent Volunteer Orientation. Volunteers make a significant contribution to our program, each adding his or her own unique talents to work with the children, parents, and teachers.

As per the discussion at that session, we are awaiting receipt of your criminal history, child abuse, and health clearances. Once you have forwarded these to the Center, we will be able to discuss your volunteer schedule with you.

We eagerly look forward to the time when you can join us at the Center. Thank you for your interest in our program.

Sincerely,


_____

Center Director

# NOTICE OF VOLUNTEER TRAINING

## Child Care Center

Dear _____:

Thank you for your interest in volunteering in our early childhood education program.

Our Volunteer Orientation Workshop will be held on _____ at _____. If you have current criminal history, child abuse, and health clearances, please bring these with you to the workshop. If you do not already have clearances, these forms will be provided for you.

Volunteers enable teachers to give much more one-on-one time to children. You are very important to the success of our program. We look forward to seeing you at orientation.

Sincerely,


_____

Center Director

# VOLUNTEER GUIDELINES

Dear Volunteer:

Welcome and thank you for giving of your time and energies to our program. The following guidelines are taken from our *Volunteer Handbook*. Please take the time to review these guidelines carefully, and discuss any questions with the classroom teachers. I am also available to support you during your volunteer time.

Sincerely,

_____

Center Director

## Key Guidelines for Center Volunteers

1. We are counting on you. If you will be late or cannot make scheduled volunteer hours, please notify the Center as soon as possible.
2. If ill with a cold or other communicable illness, please call us and stay at home.
3. When unsure of where or how to be involved, ask a classroom teacher.
4. When talking with children, stoop or sit at eye level.
5. Use a clear, expressive voice when reading to children. Hold books so that listeners can see pages. Ask occasional questions about stories.
6. If approached by parents with questions about children, please refer parents to the classroom teacher.
7. Urge children to assist with clean-up times.
8. Corporal punishment of children is prohibited. Avoid verbally shaming or embarrassing children into appropriate behavior. Refer problem behaviors to classroom teachers.

# VOLUNTEER EVALUATION

## Child Care Center

Dear Volunteer:

The attached Volunteer Evaluation provides a volunteer with documentation of service, as well as a recommendation useful for other volunteer or work activities. Thank you for your contributions to our program.

Sincerely,

_____

Center Director

**Volunteer Evaluation**

Volunteer Name _____ Length of Service _____

Evaluator _____ Title _____ Date _____

|  | | U | O | R |
|---|---|---|---|---|
| I. *Professionalism* | | | | |
| | A. Reports to Center on time on days scheduled | — | — | — |
| | B. Conforms to Center policies and procedures | — | — | — |
| | C. Displays a professional demeanor | — | — | — |
| | D. Asks questions to clarify role | — | — | — |
| | E. Seeks feedback regarding responsibilities | — | — | — |
| II. *Involvement with Children* | | | | |
| | A. Appears to enjoy involvement with children | — | — | — |
| | B. Stoops or sits at eyelevel when talking with children | — | — | — |
| | C. Uses age-appropriate language to interact with children | — | — | — |
| | D. Supports needs of individual children and group | — | — | — |
| | E. Participates in a variety of activities | — | — | — |
| III. *Involvement with Staff* | | | | |
| | A. Interacts well with staff, other volunteers | — | — | — |
| | B. Accepts authority of staff, administration | — | — | — |
| | C. Participates in staff inservice activities | — | — | — |
| | D. Contributes ideas for children's activities | — | — | — |
| | E. Supports staff initiatives | — | — | — |
| IV. *Involvement with Parents* | | | | |
| | A. Interacts well with parents, family members | — | — | — |
| | B. Observes child/family confidentiality | — | — | — |
| | C. Refers parents' questions to staff | — | — | — |
| | D. Supports parents' concerns appropriately | — | — | — |
| | E. Supports Center policies with parents | — | — | — |

Comments _____

_____

_____

_____

_____

Volunteer signature _____ Date _____

Evaluator signature _____ Date _____

*Usually, Occasionally, Rarely

# RETIRING VOLUNTEER

Dear _____:

    Congratulations on your many years of service to young children and parents. It has been a joy working with you, and observing your interactions with families and staff. Although there are always times for change, this is one instance where we would prefer not to see it. It will be difficult to find a volunteer with your commitment.

    We wish you all the best, and thank you for your many contributions to our program.

Sincerely,

_____

Center Director

# FUNDRAISING ACTIVITY: BOOK FAIR

Dear _____:

    We are pleased to inform you about an upcoming event at our Center. On _____, the celebration of World Literacy Day, from _____ until _____, we will hold our second annual Children's Book Fair. This event will feature books for children aged birth through the teen years, many in paperback format. Books will be reasonably priced to encourage purchases, and a representative from the book distribution company will be on hand to help buyers with age-appropriate selections.

    We hope that your schedule will enable you to come out to support this event, the proceeds of which will benefit the purchase of new books for the classrooms and our Lending Library.

Sincerely,


_____

Center Director

# FUNDRAISING ACTIVITY:
# BAKE-SALE PRESS RELEASE

Dear _____:

Enclosed please find a press release for publication in the next edition of the _____. Please contact me at _____ if there are any questions regarding this information.

Sincerely,


Center Director

- - - - - - - - - - - - - - - - - - - - - - - - - - - - - - -

**Press Release**

On _____ from _____ until _____, parents and staff of the _____ will hold a Bake Sale to benefit the Center's Parent Involvement component. Mouthwatering cakes, pies, doughnuts, brownies, cookies, and candies—homemade by the Center families—will be on sale at reasonable costs, along with hot and cold drinks. The community is invited to come to support this worthwhile event.

# VISIT TO ELEMENTARY SCHOOL

Dear Principal_____:

   As per our conversation of _____, I am looking forward to the visit of our Center five-year-olds to your kindergarten class. I have contacted the kindergarten teacher, _____, as per your request, and we have selected _____ for the visit to your school.

   As you know, visits like these are important to children's successful adjustment to elementary school. Teachers have been talking with the children, reading books, and practicing "kindergarten behaviors" in preparation for this transition. All are eagerly anticipating this visit.

   We value the cooperative relationship with you and your staff, and look forward to many years of positive interaction on behalf of children.

Sincerely,


_____
Center Director

# VISIT TO KINDERGARTEN CLASS

Dear _____:

   Thank you for your willingness to host a visit from our Center's five-year-olds to your kindergarten class.

   As per our conversation, 15 children and three teachers will arrive at your school at 9:30 AM, and will meet your classroom aide outside of the main office. The aide will then escort us to the kindergarten class-room. During our one-hour visit, the children will convene in a circle with your class to talk about the kindergarten experience, will hear a story read by one of our teachers, and will share snack with your class. One of our teachers will take photographs during the visit to be used during follow-up discussions with the children. We will provide your class with a set of these photographs. Our children will leave to return to the Center promptly at 10:30 AM.

   I know that this visit will alleviate many of the children's concerns about the transition to elementary school. Thank you in advance for this opportunity.

Sincerely,


_____

Center Director

# THANK-YOU
# TO KINDERGARTEN CLASS

Dear Kindergarten Friends:

We had such a wonderful time visiting your classroom on _____. Your teacher is so nice, and there were many interesting things to see and play with. We hope that you enjoyed the story that our teacher read. We thought that the snack you made for us was really delicious.

We are sending you some pictures from our visit. We hope that you like them. They remind us of our new friends in kindergarten.

Thank you!

Your friends from the _____ Class and their teachers

# REQUEST VISIT FROM KINDERGARTEN TEACHER

Dear _____:

Please accept our invitation to visit and learn more about our child care program. We have been serving the local community for many years, and a number of our graduates become pupils in your kindergarten class.

We would like to invite you to attend a Center staff meeting in order to exchange information with teachers about our curriculum and kindergarten expectations. In this way, we can better prepare children for success in your classroom. Our meetings are held weekly on Tuesdays at 1:00 PM. Please contact me _____ if your schedule will permit you to attend.

We look forward to your response.

Sincerely,

_____

Center Director

# THANK-YOU
# TO KINDERGARTEN TEACHER

## Child Care Center

Dear _____:

   We were so delighted by your visit to our Center and participation in our _____ staff meeting! Teachers are still discussing the valuable information you have shared regarding your school's goals for kindergarten students.

   Although the consensus is that we are on the right track, we are able to see some real opportunities for curriculum modification, especially with regard to helping children develop skills for kindergarten behavior and cooperation.

   Thank you for an informative and supportive visit. We hope that this is only the first of many positive exchanges between our programs.

Sincerely,


_____

Center Director

# REQUEST TO REPRESENTATIVE
# FOR SUPPORT
# OF CHILD CARE LEGISLATION

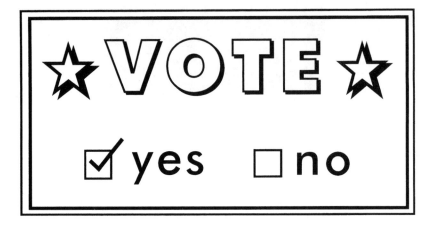

© 2002 by The Center for Applied Research in Education

Dear Representative _____:

    On _____ Bill # _____ will come before you and your colleagues in the State Legislature. As a constituent from your district, I ask that you vote to pass this important child care legislation. Many low-income families in our state do not have access to quality child care services. Passage of this legislation will provide for the establishment of many additional subsidized child care slots.

    We are counting on your vote for Bill # _____, as you will be counting on our votes in November.

Sincerely,


_____

Center Director

# THANK-YOU FOR SUPPORTING CHILD CARE LEGISLATION

Dear Representative ――――――――――:

On behalf of the children, parents, and staff of the ――――――――,
thank you for casting your support to pass Bill # ――――――. Many
young children will benefit as a result of your commitment to child care.

As you have supported our cause, we will be working to help reelect
you in the fall. When at home in your district, please come to visit our
program. We would be pleased to have you see an example of our state's
tax dollars at work.

Sincerely,


――――――――――――――
Center Director

# REQUEST FOR RFP PACKAGE
# (REQUEST FOR PROPOSAL)

## Child Care Center

Dear _____:

    I have recently become aware through the Federal Register of funds available for supporting child care staff education through ACT _____, Title _____.

    Please send us the Request for Proposal package for 2002-2003 funding. I am enclosing a brochure describing our program. If further information is required prior to issuing the RFP, please contact me at _____.

    Thank you for your consideration in this matter.

Sincerely,

_____

Center Director

Enc.

# REQUESTING FURTHER INFORMATION ABOUT A GRANT

## Child Care Center

Dear _____:

    I have recently become aware through the Federal Register of funds available for supporting child care staff education through ACT _____, Title _____.

    I am uncertain as to whether our program meets the standard for funding, and am requesting clarification of program eligibility. I am also enclosing a brochure describing our program, along with a mission statement. If further information is required to establish our program's eligibility, please contact me at _____. If you are satisfied that our program meets the criteria for funding, please forward a copy of the Request for Proposal to me at this address.

    Thank you for your consideration in this matter.

Sincerely,


_____

Center Director


Enc.

# COVER LETTER
# FOR GRANT APPLICATION

Dear _____:

I am enclosing our completed application for funds supporting child care staff education through ACT _____, Title _____. Our application includes the mandatory narrative and budget portions, as well as letters of support for our program. I understand that applicants should receive initial feedback on their proposals by _____.

If further information is required to establish our program's eligibility, please contact me at _____.

Thank you for your consideration in this matter.

Sincerely,

_____

Center Director

Enc.

# REQUEST FOR DONATION: MATERIALS

Dear _____:

We are a comprehensive child care program operating in the _____ community since _____. We provide services for children aged six months to five years, along with before- and after-school care for children six to twelve years. We presently serve fifty families.

At this time we are looking for assistance to obtain several kinds of materials for our Center, including twelve yards of colorful fabric remnants (to be used for pillows and other classroom decorations) and fifty 12″ × 12″ carpet samples (used as children's sit-upons during circle and story times). I am aware that your company sells these products, and hope to persuade you to donate these items to us.

I am enclosing a brochure that provides additional information about ourpProgram, and invite you to visit our Center and observe our activities first-hand. Please contact me at your convenience at _____ to discuss my request.

Thank you for your consideration in this matter.

Sincerely,


_____
Center Director


Enc.

# REQUEST FOR DONATION: FUNDS

Dear _____:

We are a comprehensive child care program operating in the _____ community since _____. We provide services for children aged six months to five years, along with before- and after-school care for children six to twelve years. We presently serve fifty families.

At this time we are looking for assistance to purchase new playground equipment for our children. As you may have noticed in passing the Center, our present equipment has seen better days and is in danger of becoming a hazard to the children. I hope to convince your company to bear the tax-deductible cost of replacing this equipment and creating a safer environment for many of the neighborhood's children.

I have drawn up a prospectus describing the equipment that I plan to purchase, its cost, and the cost of installation. Also enclosed are the ratings for this equipment from the Consumer Product Safety Commission.

A brochure providing additional information about our program is included, and I invite you to visit our Center and observe our activities first-hand. Please contact me at your convenience at _____ to further discuss my request.

Thank you for your consideration in this matter.

Sincerely,


_____
Center Director

Enc.

© 2002 by The Center for Applied Research in Education

# REQUEST FOR DONATION: SERVICES

Dear _____ :

   We are a comprehensive child care program operating in the _____ community since _____. We provide services for children aged six months to five years, along with before- and after-school care for children six to twelve years. We presently serve fifty families.

   At this time we are looking for legal assistance to review the Center's contracts and other forms. Many of these were developed when the Program first opened and may not meet current legal standards. As a nonprofit agency we are unable to afford legal fees, and hope that you will consider donating your services. I anticipate that ten hours of your time would be needed for meetings with our Advisory Board and review of our current contracts and forms.

   I am enclosing a brochure that provides additional information about our program, and invite you to visit our Center and observe our activities first-hand. Please contact me at your convenience at _____ to discuss my request.

   Thank you for your consideration in this matter.

Sincerely,


_____
Center Director

Enc.

# THANK-YOU
# FOR DONATED MATERIALS

## Child Care Center

Dear _____:

On behalf of the families and staff of _____, thank you for your very generous donation of twenty yards of beautiful fabric remnants and five books of carpet samples to our program. Our children surely have the very best pillows, murals, and sit-upons in town!

I would like to renew our invitation for you to visit our Center, especially since we have made fine use of your donated materials. We will also keep you apprised of Center events by way of our monthly newsletter.

Thank you once again for supporting our program.

Sincerely,

_____

Center Director

# INVITATION
# TO ALUMNI FAMILIES EVENT

Dear Alumni Family:

We are pleased to invite you to our Second Annual Alumni Families Picnic. The picnic will be held in _____ on _____ from _____ until _____. As you will remember if you were with us last year, the park provides grills, and we will be serving hot dogs, hamburgers, salads, and fresh fruit. Any family wishing to contribute a dessert for this event is welcome to do so, and should advise the main office of the treat they plan to bring.

We are certain that this event will provide another opportunity to renew old friendships and make new ones. The park has a playground that the children will enjoy. Restroom facilities are near the picnic area, and are clean and well stocked.

In order for us to plan for the number of families attending, please contact the Center no later than _____ at _____ with the count of persons who will attend the Picnic.

Thank you once again for your ongoing support of our program.

Sincerely,

_____

Center Director

# KEEPING TRACK
# OF ALUMNI FAMILIES

Dear Alumni Family:

We hope that this letter finds your family in good health and circumstances. All of our families, present and past, are important to us. Every year we ask our alumni families to provide us with an update of their addresses and any changes or additions to families.

Please take a few minutes to complete and return the tear-off portion of this letter and return it to us in the stamped, self-addressed envelope by _____.
This year we are compiling an *Alumni Family Directory* and would like to include your family information. If you do not want to be included in the *Directory*, please indicate this on the attached form.

Thank you for your continuing support of our program.

Sincerely,


_____
Center Director

- - - - - - - - - - - - - - - - - - - - - - - - - - - - - - - - -

### Alumni Family Update

Family name _____ Parent(s) names _____

Address _____

Child or children who attended the program _____

Years children attended program _____

Changes or additions to family _____

____ We **do** want to be included in the *Alumni Family Directory*

____ We **do not** want to be included in the *Alumni Family Directory*

# PROGRAM UPDATE FOR ALUMNI FAMILIES

**Child Care Center**

Dear Alumni Family:

It is with reluctance that I advise you that as of _____ I will no longer be the director of _____. I have accepted a position as director of _____. Although it is difficult to leave all of the children, families, and staff at our Center, the new job is a wonderful opportunity for me to develop new skills.

_____ has been offered the position of Director of our Center. She has extensive credentials and experience, and will bring a breath of fresh air to the program. We have talked about the close relationship with alumni families, and the new director will continue to support this link.

As for me, I will see you at the annual alumni picnic!

My very best wishes to your family, and thank you for your continuing support of our program.

Sincerely,


_____

Center Director

# LETTER TO THE EDITOR #1

## Child Care Center

To the Editor:

On behalf of the children, families, and staff of _____, thank you for the excellent article in the _____ edition of the newspaper on the state of our city's child care facilities. The article precisely described the differences between those programs accredited by the National Association for the Education of Young Children and those that lack credentialing. The inclusion of testimony from parents about the services they receive at accredited facilities provided information about quality indicators that can be used by families searching for child care services.

If the condition of programs for young children is to be upgraded, there must be public access to accurate information about the field. We commend your reporter and newspaper for taking time to research and publish accurate and supportive information about child care.

Sincerely,

_____
Center Director

# LETTER TO THE EDITOR #2

To the Editor:

I am writing in response to the Letter to the Editor from _____ _____ published in the _____ edition of your newspaper. I am always dismayed to read inaccurate information about child care and the families that use these services. Child care and early education are no longer "welfare services."

Although many low-income families, and others with parents pursuing training or education, receive subsidized services, many families bear the full cost of child care. According to the web-based Forum on Child and Family Statistics, 60% of children aged three to six years were in some type of center-based child care situation in 1999. This data does not include children in family child care or home-based settings. The Forum further indicates that highly educated parents were more likely to seek out preschool programs for their children. Given the recent research on early brain development and the significance of an early start to learning, it is little wonder that the most effective parents choose quality comprehensive early childhood programs for their young children.

Rather than demeaning the use of child care and related programs, we should be applauding those who have made a career of work with young children.

Sincerely,

_____
Center Director

# ARRANGING FIELD VISIT TO COMMUNITY SITE

Dear _____:

Thank you for agreeing to host a visit by the four-year-old children from our Center. The children have been learning about fire safety as a part of the curriculum. A visit to the fire station to meet and talk with firefighters and to see the trucks and equipment will help the children further understand the importance of your work in safeguarding the community.

We will arrive at the firehouse promptly at 10:00 AM on _____. There will be 15 children in the group and three teachers. As per our conversation, we are planning a visit of one-half hour. The children are really looking forward to this field trip. Thank you for making your firefighters available to meet with the children.

Sincerely,

_____
Center Director

# THANK-YOU FOR VISIT TO COMMUNITY SITE

Dear Firefighters of Engine Company # _____:

Thank you for letting us visit your firehouse. The fire engines are really big and red. We wanted to slide down the fire pole, but you said we might get hurt. We liked trying on the fire boots and hats. We liked the fire dog the best. He was very friendly and cute.

We are sending you some pictures we drew of our visit to your firehouse. Please come and visit us at our Center.

Your friends,

Children and Teachers from _____

# NOTICE OF EVENT:
# THANKSGIVING FEAST

© 2002 by The Center for Applied Research in Education

Dear _____ :

    Please join us for a Thanksgiving Feast to be held at the Center on Wednesday, November _____ from _____ until _____. The children have been working for several weeks preparing traditional foods and desserts for this event. Our families are providing paper goods and desserts. This promises to be an occasion of celebration and thanksgiving for us all.

    Please come to celebrate with us. We hope to see you there.

Sincerely,

_____

Center Director

# NOTICE OF EVENT: JULY 4th PICNIC

Dear _____:

    We are pleased to invite friends of the Center to a July 4th picnic, to be held at _____ from _____ until _____.

    The Center is supplying hot dogs, hamburgers, rolls, condiments, sodas, and paper goods, and parents are providing side dishes. If you are able to attend as our guest and enjoy the day with us, please contact the Center at _____.

    We hope you are free to celebrate the 4th of July with us!

Sincerely,


_____

Center Director

# NOTICE OF EVENT:
# SPRING FASHION SHOW

Dear _____:

    Once again our Center is hosting a Spring Fashion Show featuring parents, children, and staff dressed in their spring finery. The Spring Fashion Show will be held on the evening of Saturday, _____, from _____ until _____. The cost of tickets is _____ at the door and includes refreshments. Proceeds will benefit the purchase of new classroom computers at the Center. Please tell others about this special event.

    Please come out and join us for a much anticipated and festive afternoon!

Sincerely,

_____

Center Director

# NOTICE OF EVENT: CENTER READ-IN

Dear _____:

    In an effort to promote family literacy, the Center is hosting a day-long Read-In on _____ from _____ until _____. Parents, teachers, volunteers, and friends of the Center will be reading to and conducting language arts activities throughout the day with our children. While the infants and toddlers will take their regular nap time, three- to five-year-olds and school-aged children will participate throughout the day.

    The Center will provide snacks and lunch for families and visitors. To indicate your participation in the Read-In, please complete the tear-off section below and return it to the Center, or call us at _____.

    We hope to see you at the Read-In!

Sincerely,


_____
Center Director

------------------------------------------------------------

### Read-In Response Form

____ I plan to be there to participate in the Center Read-In on _____.
I will be volunteering my time from:

    ____ 9:00–11:00 AM      ____ 11:00 AM–1:00 PM

    ____ 1:00–3:00 PM      ____ 3:00–5:00 PM

____ I will be unable to participate in the Center Read-In.

Respondent signature _____ Date _____

# EARLY CHILDHOOD CENTERS' JOINT FIELD TRIP

Dear _____ :

I am so pleased that our programs have begun working closely together. I feel that I have a genuine and compassionate colleague with whom to share administrative issues and ideas. Our children, families, and staff will also benefit from the events we have planned.

As per our conversation, our Zoo trip is scheduled for _____ at _____. I will be contacting the Zoo regarding ticket purchase at group rates, and you will be handling transportation arrangements with the bus company. Our Center's cook is preparing peanut butter and cheese sandwiches to accompany us on the trip, and your Center will arrange for fruit and drinks for the children. Each of our centers will provide its own identification tags for the children, tissues, wipes, first-aid kits, cameras, etc.

We will be sending a request to parents regarding volunteers needed for the day. We can talk further before the trip to assess whether supervision by adults is adequately addressed.

Looking forward to a great field trip!

Sincerely,

_____

Center Director

# EARLY CHILDHOOD CENTERS' STAFF EXCHANGE PROGRAM

## Child Care Center

Dear ————————————:

    I was so pleased to know that you share my enthusiasm for the staff-exchange program concept! It is a wonderful way to expose staff to new curriculum ideas and to create a support network for them.

    As per our agreement, we will begin by introducing the exchange idea at staff meetings at our respective centers next week. We will then meet to discuss reactions to the plan. Any staff member who is strongly resistant to the exchange program will not be required to participate. Having answered staff concerns adequately, we can begin the exchange program on a trial basis next month.

    The plan we outlined will include a week-long exchange experience for each teaching staff member. Staff will be exchanged one per center per week. Each staff person participating in the exchange will go to a same developmental/age group classroom as he/she normally serves in. Exchanged staff are not expected to act as lead teachers in the programs they visit, but will support the plans created by the home staff for that week. When exchange staff arrive at the beginning of the visiting period, they will be met and apprised of the plans for the week by a host staff member. That individual will also answer any questions that the visitor may have about the program. During the exchange, staff will receive their full salaries and benefits. We have checked to assure that our insurance policies will cover any injuries to staff that might occur during the course of the exchange program. We will talk weekly to assess the success of the program.

    I am convinced that many staff will receive this plan enthusiastically. Thank you so much for your openness to new ideas!

Sincerely,


————————————————

Center Director

# EARLY CHILDHOOD PROGRAMS'
# DUAL INSERVICE

## Child Care Center

Dear _____:

We are so fortunate to have acquired the services of _____ to provide an inservice training for our staff members. This trainer is known for his knowledge of the field and for his ability to communicate with a broad range of individuals. Although my program would not ordinarily have been able to afford this trainer's fee, working together with your program makes the cost manageable.

As we have planned, the inservice is scheduled for _____ at _____ at our Center. The topic selected is one about which my staff members have consistently requested additional information. This is sure to be interesting and beneficial training.

Thanks so very much for your support and cooperation!

Sincerely,


_____

Center Director

# EARLY CHILDHOOD CENTERS' PARTICIPATION IN CONFERENCE WORKSHOP

Dear _____:

I am looking forward to our joint workshop at the National Association for the Education of Young Children Conference in Washington, DC on _____. We have put so much time and energy into our preparation that I feel confident our presentation will be well received.

As we have planned, I will meet you at _____ on _____ to depart for Washington. I appreciate having a colleague with whom to share what I have learned, and I value the opportunity to contribute our expertise to others in the profession.

Sincerely,

_____

Center Director

# MEMBERSHIP IN EARLY CHILDHOOD ORGANIZATION

Dear ⸻:

Enclosed please find a check in the amount of ⸻ for my enrollment as a member in Association of Childhood Education International. I understand that my membership entitles me to the association's journal, as well as membership in a local association chapter.

I would like my business address used for my membership; accordingly, please see the letterhead address. My business telephone number is ⸻.

Thank you for your assistance in this matter.

Sincerely,

⸻
Center Director

Enc.

# ADVERTISEMENT: CENTER DIRECTOR

Dear _____:

Please include the following advertisement in the weekend (Friday, Saturday, and Sunday) employment sections of the newspaper. In adherence with your rates, I am enclosing a check to cover the cost of the ad. I can be contacted at _____ if further information is required.

*Director—comprehensive child care program serving young children and families. Minimum Bachelor's degree in ECE, five years' teaching/administrative experience. Send vitae and requirements to _____.*

Sincerely,

_____

Center Director

Enc.

# ADVERTISEMENT: LEAD TEACHER

Dear _____:

Please include the following advertisement in the weekend (Friday, Saturday, and Sunday) employment sections of the newspaper. In adherence with your rates, I am enclosing a check to cover the cost of the ad. I can be contacted at _____ if further information is required.

*Lead Teacher—for four-year-olds in comprehensive child car- setting. Responsible for curriculum planning. Minimum Associate's Degree in ECE, three years' experience. Send current resume and requirements to _____.*

Sincerely,


_____

Center Director

Enc.

# ADVERTISEMENT: TEACHER'S AIDE

Dear _____:

    Please include the following advertisement in the weekend (Friday, Saturday, and Sunday) employment sections of the newspaper. In adherence with your rates, I am enclosing a check to cover the cost of the ad. I can be contacted at _____ if further information is required.

*Teacher's Aide—for three-year-olds in comprehensive child care setting. Responsible for assisting teacher in implementing children's program. Minimum Child Development Associate Credential, three years' experience in early childhood education setting. Send current resume and requirements to _____.*

Sincerely,

_____
Center Director

Enc.

# RECEIPT OF NAEYC ACCREDITATION

## Child Care Center

Dear Advisory Board Members and Friends of the Center:

For the past nine months, our Center's administration and staff have been involved in an extensive self-study as part of the process necessary for center accreditation by the National Association for the Education of Young Children. The self-study was an arduous but worthwhile process requiring us to examine our performance in areas that include: the safety of the environment, adult–child interactions, and appropriateness of the curriculum.

I am proud to announce that on _____ validators from the National Academy of Early Childhood Education Programs awarded our program NAEYC Accreditation! Accreditation indicates that our Center meets standards for the highest quality programs for young children, far exceeding those mandated for state licensing. Our accreditation is valid for three years, at which time we will once again enter into a self-study.

I am proud of the involvement and participation of our staff and families in this process, and know that you, too, will want to applaud this achievement.

Sincerely,

_____

Center Director

# COMMUNITY EVALUATION

## Child Care Center

Dear Advisory Board Members and Friends of the Center:

In an effort to improve the quality of services to children and parents, we are asking Board Members, volunteers, and other friends who regularly observe the program to complete the attached Community Evaluation of Child Care Services. This form will take only a few minutes of your time, but will provide us with valuable information to offer the best possible program. Complete this evaluation anonymously and return it to the Center in the enclosed stamped, self-addressed envelope, or to the main office no later than _____.

Thank you in advance for your time.

Sincerely,

_____

Center Director

- - - - - - - - - - - - - - - - - - - - - - - - - - - - - - -

**Community Evaluation of Child Care Services**

Directions: Indicate your response to survey questions by circling the answer that applies.

When I visit the Center . . .

| | | | |
|---|---|---|---|
| 1. | . . . staff are generally professional and courteous. | YES | NO |
| 2. | . . . parents are treated with concern and respect. | YES | NO |
| 3. | . . . children seem busy and content. | YES | NO |
| 4. | . . . staff interact pleasantly and cooperatively. | YES | NO |
| 5. | . . . materials and equipment appear in good repair. | YES | NO |
| 6. | . . . environments seem safe and healthy. | YES | NO |
| 7. | . . . children appear to be learning from activities. | YES | NO |
| 8. | . . . the telephone is answered in a professional manner. | YES | NO |

Comments/Recommended improvements _____

_____

_____

# ARRANGING LIBRARY VISIT

Dear _____ :

Thank you for talking with me by telephone about our child care center. We are pleased to have entered into a relationship with the Free Library. Our program philosophy stresses the importance of child and family literacy, and we are looking forward to utilizing the children's division of the library. Accordingly, on _____ at _____ our children's groups (toddler, preschool, and school age) will make weekly visits for Story Hour. As per our conversation, teachers will be able to select and check out up to 15 books to bring back to the Center. These will be returned to the Library on the next visit.

We appreciate this opportunity to include additional books and literacy experiences in our curriculum.

Sincerely,


_____
Center Director

# CHILD CARE NEEDS ASSESSMENT

## Child Care Center

Dear _____:

Our child care center is in the process of determining the need for additional classrooms at our site to serve infants and toddlers. Please take a few moments of your valuable time to complete the attached survey, and return it to us in the enclosed stamped, self-addressed envelope. Your quick response will give us important input into the need for these services.

Thank you for your consideration in this matter.

Sincerely,

_____

Center Director

- - - - - - - - - - - - - - - - - - - - - - - - - - - -

### Child Care Needs Assessment

Please circle your response to the following questions.

1. Do you have an infant child living in your home?                      YES      NO
2. Do you have a toddler living in your home?                            YES      NO
3. If you have an infant or toddler, do you currently use any
   form of child care services?                                         YES      NO
4. If NO, would you consider child care if high-quality,
   affordable care was available?                                       YES      NO
5. If currently using child care, this care is (circle one):
   Home-based          Center-based          Provided by family
6. Are you pleased with your current child care services?               YES      NO
7. Would you consider changing your present child-
   care situation?                                                      YES      NO
8. What range of fees would you pay for quality child care
   for your infant or toddler? Costs are weekly. (Circle one)
   $50–$75                 $75–$150                 $150–$200

Thank you for your assistance with this survey!

FIGURE 4.1

# CENTER NEWSLETTER

## The caring word . . .

Child Care Center

July 2003                                              Volume 2, Number 1

### From the Director's Chair

We are so proud to announce receipt of our Center Accreditation from NAEYC! We now rate as among the best of programs in the nation. We had to meet exacting standards and pass inspection by national validators, but we have made the grade! Thanks to all parents, Board members, and staff who played a role in this achievement.

### Success of Alumni Families Picnic

The annual Alumni Families Picnic was held at Grove Park on June 25. Twenty families attended the event, sharing stories about the Center, staff, and their growing children. The sandbox, swings, and wading pools provided entertainment for more than forty children in attendance. Commented Emily Pullan, age 12, class of 1995, "It was an exciting day. It was fun to see my old friends again." We are all looking forward to next year's picnic.

### Congratulations Are in Order . . .

To Alyson Watkins and Craig Murphy and Gayle and David Jenkins who are expecting babies this summer . . . To staff member Kathy Hornberger who received her Bachelor's Degree from Beaver College . . . To Patty Regina, Joan Brennan, and Wesley Munchus who celebrated birthdays this month . . . To the Monroe Family who welcomed little Courtney Alyssa into the world on May 8.

### Reminder About Zoo Trip

The trip to the Philadelphia Zoo is planned for Tuesday, July 30. Buses will depart the Center promptly at 9:00 AM and will return at 3:00 PM. Trip fees are $5 for children and $7 for adults. Fees are due in the main office no later than July 15.

### A Warning About Car Seats

The Consumer Product Safety Commission has issued a recall for the Baby Seat Car Seat Model #0001. The seat straps can release during a crash. Call 555-5555 to get a repair kit if you have this car seat.

### Staff-Exchange Program to Begin

In September a Staff-Exchange Program with Runabouts Child Care Center will begin. Each week our Center will have a visiting teacher from Runabouts. A teacher from our Center will be working at Runabouts during that same week. The visiting teacher will be treated as a member of our staff, working with the children and attending staff meetings. Parents should continue to address their questions to the regular teachers, who know the children best. The Exchange Program is designed to expose teachers to new curriculum and activity ideas. After their one-week visits are concluded, teachers will return to their regular classrooms. Please stop into the office with any questions about the Exchange Program.

### Passage of Child Care Legislation

Many parents and staff participated in the letters campaign to support the passage of Bill #555 in the State Legislature. On June 1 the Legislature passed this important bill. As a result there will be funds available to subsidize child care for many additional families. Congratulations to us all!

### P.S.

Don't forget to support the local legislators who supported the passage of Bill #555.

FIGURE 4.2

# ANNUAL REPORT
# TO PARENTS, STAFF,
# BOARD MEMBERS, AND COMMUNITY

## Annual Report—July 2003

I. *A New School Year*

As our Center begins its 10th year of operation, our funding is guaranteed for the next three years, enrollments are up, and staff turnover is down. We have an energetic parents' group and a supportive Advisory Board. This said, we must move forward during this year in a number of areas. Our curriculum is in need of modification, and there is need for new playground equipment. This month the search will begin for a new Center Director, as the current director will move on to a new position. We are also beginning a series of new interactions with a nearby program, Runabouts Child Care Center. These are designed primarily for staff support and development, an area of our program that needs more work. Overall, we have a program that is functioning well, and the outlook for the upcoming year is an excellent one.

II. *Center Leadership*

The present director has been administering the Center for five years. She has recently made the decision to take a position with the State Department of Education in the fall. With oversight from the Advisory Board, advertisements have already been placed in local newspapers and on the DVAEYC web-based jobs board. If a qualified administrator can be identified in the next month, there will be another 30 days during which the transfer of information and orientation of the new director can be conducted by the current director.

III. *Center Enrollments*

Center enrollments are up. As of this report, all 50 slots for child care are filled by eligible children. Additionally, there is a waiting list of 15 children.

IV. *Plan of Action*

There are plans for 2003-04 to make programmatic changes in the following areas:

A. Curriculum modification—Two curriculum training specialists will be conducting sessions with the Center staff during the months of September and October. The purpose of this training will be to examine the current curriculum, identify problem areas, and make necessary modifications.

B. Playground equipment—An appeal to Progressive Pharmacies, a local company with close ties to the community, has resulted in a grant to purchase and install new playground equipment. Installation will begin later this month.

FIGURE 4.2 (*continued*)

C. Staff Development—The relationship with Runabouts Child Care Center will include the following activities during the upcoming months: A field trip jointly planned and implemented by both centers; a dual staff inservice addressing the promotion of appropriate behavior in young children; a staff exchange program (see attached memo for details); and a joint presentation by the centers' directors at the upcoming NAEYC conference.

## IV. *Center Performance*

The Center has been awarded accreditation by the Academy for Early Childhood Programs, an arm of National Association for the Education of Young Children. Accreditation resulted from an extensive self study and visits from Academy validators. This credential is valid for three years, at which time the Center will apply to renew our accreditation.

## V. *Technology*

Since the purchase of two Macintosh computers in the Fall of 2001, the Center has been successful in putting all essential forms and new records on CD-Rom. Clerical staff are continuing the process of putting older records on diskettes, and expect to complete this process by Spring of 2003.

## VI. *Facilities*

With the change in maintenance staff in March of 2002, there has been a steady increase in Center cleanliness and overall health conditions. Our new maintenance engineer has been successful in bringing in an effective pest control company, and has instituted new and efficient procedures for maintaining the appearance and condition of classrooms.

## VII. *Awards and Grants*

In addition to the grant for playground equipment from Progressive Pharmacies, our Center has received funds from Walker and Walker Attorneys-at-Law for full-day child care scholarships for two children and one school-age scholarship for one-year periods. This firm began its involvement with us through our volunteer program.

## VIII. *School Year Calendar*

The following Center holidays will be observed in 2002-203:

- Independence Day—July 4
- Labor Day—September 3
- Thanksgiving Holiday—November 21 and 22
- Winter Holidays—December 24–January 1
- Martin Luther King, Jr. Birthday—January 17
- Presidents' Day—February 21
- Spring Holidays—April 9–April 15
- Memorial Day—May 30

# CHILD CARE HERO AWARD

**Child Care Center**

Dear _____:

On behalf of our child care center and the community, thank you for the commitment you have demonstrated to child care and early childhood education. Due in large part to your fundraising efforts, we have been able to purchase new playground equipment and make repairs to our Center that enabled us to complete the process for Accreditation by the National Association for the Education of Young Children. Although a volunteer, you have consistently committed your time and energy to addressing the needs of our children.

Accordingly, you are designated a "Child Care Hero," and we present you this certificate and extend our gratitude in acknowledgment of your work on behalf of children.

Sincerely,

_____

Center Director

FIGURE 4.3

# CHILD CARE HERO CERTIFICATE

FIGURE 4.4

# ADVISORY BOARD MEMBER CERTIFICATE

Advisory Board Member

Teacher

Director

FIGURE 4.5

# CHILD CARE VOLUNTEER
# CERTIFICATE

**Child-Care Volunteer**

_Director_

_Teacher_

# Letters to Consultants and Contractors

Early childhood directors frequently utilize outside resources to support the efforts of their programs. Some of these resources include consultants,* who assist in the implementation of services to children, and staff developers whose function is to train and inform parents and/or individuals employed at the center. Although these services can be costly and outside the means of some programs, there are community colleges, teaching hospitals, and education and human service resources that can be obtained free or at a low cost.

Obtaining the input of outside experts must be handled in a professional manner. With the widespread interest in child care, there is a sudden proliferation of "experts." A consultant should be asked for a curriculum vitae and references from previous clients. A contract should be drawn up, and all arrangements for services should be in writing, including the services to be performed; the day, date, and time; the degree of satisfaction expected at conclusion; the timetable involved; and the amount the consultant is to be paid for his/her work. After services have been rendered, a consultant should receive a follow-up letter that includes feedback on the effectiveness of the consultation.

A wide range of professional resources are available to support early childhood programs. Health checks of children's teeth, hearing, or eyes can be provided by local hospitals, clinics, or private practitioners. If children are suspected of having extraordinary health or behavioral needs, there are agencies in all states whose role is to screen children for problems and to link them with appropriate intervention.

Consultants can be employed to provide parent education and staff training. Although a program director may feel capable of selecting topics for both populations, it is generally best to consult trainers regarding their needs or special interests. It is a waste of valuable funds to bring in an expert in whom no one is interested. Once parents and staff have contributed their ideas for training, a director should prioritize the requests before seeking a consultant. Others can also be asked for their input regarding trainers. Staff attending college or professional conferences may have learned about speakers who would better meet the needs of their agency.

*This section contains some fictitious names and addresses to suggest possible sources of services.

When scheduling consultant services, directors should consider the convenience of those receiving the services. A specialist coming to screen a child for delays should be asked to visit in the morning hours, when children are most likely to be alert. Staff training should generally be conducted early in the week, during working hours. Children's nap times are opportune for inservice activities.

Parents should be asked about the times best for them to attend meetings. In the absence of any consensus, activities for parents should be arranged at various times throughout the year. Thus, all families have some opportunity to attend.

Early childhood programs also utilize the services of contractors,* individuals who provide equipment and materials, installations, repairs, and maintenance. These are services without which an agency cannot survive. However, working with contractors can be complex, further complicated when a director is unsophisticated about service processes or equipment. Although many contractors are reputable and fair, it is essential to obtain a detailed contract for services, to study it carefully, and clarify any discrepancies. Administrators should seriously consider obtaining legal assistance to review contracts for loopholes and ambiguous language.

Directors should never presume to have all the necessary skills or answers for program effectiveness. The best schools for young children welcome outsiders, who bring innovative ideas and cognitive, emotional, and physical change, and who keep programs changing along with the needs of families and staff.

---

*This section contains some fictitious names and addresses to suggest possible sources of services.

# SEEKING SPECIAL SERVICES: PSYCHOLOGIST

## Child Care Center

Dr. Jennifer Sweet
Child Psychologist
410 N. Broad Street
Anytown, PA 11111

Dear Dr. Sweet:

As per our telephone conversation on March 15, I am seeking the services of a consultant to evaluate the behavior of a child in our child care program. This child, a male, age five years, has recently exhibited a change in behavior. While previously eager to talk with staff and other children, and willing to engage in a wide range of activities, he has become tearful and no longer engages with the other children.

His parents are also concerned about obvious differences in his inter-actions with others, and they have given their permission for a specialist to observe their child and to make recommendations. They have also signed a release form granting permission for a specialist to review records kept by the caregiving staff.

It is my understanding that you will be able to meet with the child's parents and myself during the week of April 1 to further determine how you can assist us in this matter and that there will be no fee until you determine your ability to work with us.

Thank you for talking with me and for your willingness to work fur-ther with us. I look forward to meeting with you.

Sincerely,

_____

Center Director

# SEEKING SPECIAL SERVICES: AUDIOLOGIST

Clinic Directorc
Audiology Clinic
211 N. Main Street
Anytown, PA 11111

Dear Clinic Director:

I am the director of a child care center serving 50 children ages two to five years. I am writing to you at the suggestion of Dr. Wilma Davis, who serves on our Policy Board. As you know, the early years are essential for the development of children's spoken language and other communication skills. It is for this reason that I am seeking expert audiology services to screen the hearing of the children attending our program.

As we are a nonprofit agency, our funds for such services are extremely limited. I am hoping that you will consider conducting a free or low-cost annual screening for us. It is my hope that those children who may have hearing problems can be identified at as early an age as possible, enabling them to receive immediate intervention.

I invite you to visit our center and to meet the children and staff. At that time, I would be pleased to discuss  further with you the possibility of a screening for the children. I can be reached at _____.

Thank you for your consideration in this matter.

Sincerely,

_____

Center Director

© 2002 by The Center for Applied Research in Education

# SEEKING SPECIAL SERVICES: PEDIATRIC DENTAL SERVICES

Margaret Stewart, Coordinator
Dental Hygiene Program
Anytown Community College
111 W. Market Street
Anytown, PA 11111

Dear Ms. Stewart:

I am the director of a child care center serving 50 preschool children and families. I am interested in helping our families, some of whom are low income, to obtain a range of health-screening services. I have found that unless children have tooth pain, many parents feel that dental screening and hygiene services are unnecessary for children with primary teeth. As a consequence, some of our children have decayed and prematurely lost teeth.

I understand that your Dental Hygiene Program prepares students interested in pediatric dental hygiene, and that some community-involvement activities are required for graduation (as per the description in the college catalog). I would like to suggest forming a linkage with our child care center to provide a setting for a practicum experience for your students. Our teaching staff would welcome your students' input regarding dental care and nutrition activities for the children, as well as the possibility of a semiannual cleaning and screening of children's teeth. We are aware that your students are still learning, and oversight from one of your faculty would be required. We would refer parents to a dentist upon your recommendation.

I would appreciate the opportunity to meet with you to further discuss this proposal. I can be reached at _____ during business hours. Thank you for your consideration in this matter.

Sincerely,


_____
Center Director

# SEEKING SPECIAL SERVICES: PEDIATRIC SUPPORT

Dr. Denise King
Anytown Pediatric Group
666 Broadway
Anytown, PA 11111

Dear Dr. King:

It was a pleasure meeting and talking with you at the monthly meeting of Anytown Association for the Education of Young Children. It is exciting to know that you and your colleagues are taking a strong interest in child care.

Many of the children in our child care center do not receive regular pediatric services, and when they are ill their parents seek care for them through the hospital emergency room. I am interested in increasing the frequency of well-child care among our families, and would appreciate any information that you could provide, pharmaceutical pamphlets, posters, or other, that we could display at the Center. I am also interested in having you address our parents' group at one of their regular meetings. Our meetings are held monthly on a rotating schedule of mornings, late afternoons, and evenings. I hope that your schedule will permit a speaking engagement. We are able to offer a small honorarium for your services.

I will contact your office during the week of July 29 to talk with your scheduling staff. If you would prefer to contact me, I can be reached during business hours at _____. In the meantime, feel free to come and visit our program. The hours are 7:00 AM to 6:00 PM Monday through Friday.

Thank you for your consideration in this matter.

Sincerely,


_____

Center Director

# SEEKING SPECIAL SERVICES: SPEECH THERAPIST

Linda Macon, Supervising Speech Therapist
Anytown Children's Special Services
500 E. Market Street
Anytown, PA 11111

Dear Ms. Macon:

As per our conversation of October 15, the report from the Audiology Clinic confirms a moderate hearing loss in James Smith, a four-year-old male child attending our Center. I am enclosing a release signed by James's parents, and a copy of the audiologist's report. In early November, James will have the surgery to insert drainage tubes into his middle ears. When he returns to the Center the following week, we have planned, along with his parents, that he will begin speech therapy.

It is my understanding that a member of your staff will come to our child care center for one hour, twice weekly, to work with James. We will make our classroom equipment and materials available for use by the assigned speech therapist. I also understand that the cost of the therapy is covered by the Anytown School District under provisions for special education for children under kindergarten age. When James enters kindergarten next fall, he will be assigned a speech therapist by the school district.

I will contact you as soon as we know the date of James's expected return to the Center. I can be reached at _____ if you need to speak with me prior to that time.

Thank you for your assistance in responding to the needs of our children.

Sincerely,

_____
Center Director

# SEEKING SPECIAL SERVICES: FAMILY THERAPIST

Robert Marks, Ph.D.
Anytown Family Therapy Center
213 King Drive
Anytown, PA 11111

Dear Dr. Marks:

I have recently learned of your Anytown Family Therapy Center, and the high praise you have received for providing quality, reasonable-cost and/or sliding-scale services to families in our community.

As a child care center director, I often come into contact with families experiencing discord or trauma, and I would like to be able to refer parents to local resources. If you have a brochure describing your facility, I would be pleased to display and to distribute it to those families who would benefit from your services.

We would also like to invite you to visit our Center, and to learn more about our services to children and parents. Feel free to contact me at your convenience at _____. I look forward to hearing from you.

Sincerely,


_____
Center Director

© 2002 by The Center for Applied Research in Education

# SEEKING SPECIAL SERVICES: DRUG AND ALCOHOL COUNSELING

Child Care Center

Carolyn Lark, M.S.W.
Anytown Drug & Alcohol Recovery
444 Broad Street
Anytown, PA 11111

Dear Ms. Lark:

We are a community-based child care center providing services for infants, toddlers, preschoolers, and school-age children and their parents. Many of our client and staff families have reported problems with drug and alcohol abuse. We are aware that addiction is a widespread problem, and want to create networks with local agencies that can assist our agency families.

I am aware of the fine reputation of your program, and would like to arrange a visit to your site in order to learn more about the exent of your services. In turn, I hope that you will visit our Center to speak to our parents and staff. I will contact your office in the upcoming week to schedule an appointment at your convenience.

I look forward to meeting with you.

Sincerely,


_____
Center Director

# CONSULTANT: SEEKING INFORMATION ABOUT

## Child Care Center

Alyson B. Watkins, M.S.W.
Director
Alyson's Child Care Center
747 Broad Street
Anytown, PA 11111

Dear Alyson:

Our Center has been looking for a consultant to work with staff on modifying our classroom environments to better serve our children. One of the consultants contacted was Marta Ames, who listed you as a reference. I understand that Ms. Ames has conducted workshops for your staff, and would appreciate your feedback on the success of these sessions. I am particularly interested in the degree of Ms. Ames's rapport with a wide range of individuals, and the extent of her knowledge about the field.

Please contact me at _____ if there is information you are willing to share with me. Thank you for your consideration in this matter.

Sincerely,

_____
Center Director

# CONSULTANT: FIRE SAFETY

## Child Care Center

Community Service Representative
Anytown Fire Department
999 Market Street
Anytown, PA 11111

Sir/Madam:

Our child care center serves 50 children and parents in our community. Recently, one of our families lost their home in a catastrophic fire. They very nearly lost their lives.

I am interested in having a fire department representative visit our Center to discuss fire safety in the home and at the Center. I have heard news reports indicating that appliances and electrical wiring are major causes of fires. I know that parents and staff would be interested in the latest on these hazards, as well as facts on smoke detectors.

Our parents' group meets once each month on the first Tuesday. I hope that a firefighter will be able to arrange to meet with us sometime in the next few months. I will contact your office soon as a follow-up to this communication.

Thank you for your consideration in this matter.

Sincerely,

_____

Center Director

# CONSULTANT: PROGRAM EVALUATOR

## Child Care Center

Alyson B. Watkins, M.S.W.
Director
Alyson's Child Care Center
747 Broad Street
Anytown, PA 11111

Dear Alyson:

As you know, two years ago our program received its first National Association for the Education of Young Children Accreditation. The time has passed quickly, and we will need to apply for reaccreditation next year. As a director who has successfully completed this process several times, an objective professional, and a colleague whose input I greatly value, I hope to persuade you to conduct an observation of our program and to provide feedback on areas for Center improvement. Three hours of observation in our classrooms should afford you with ample information. We are able to offer you a small honorarium for your services.

I hope that your very busy schedule will permit you to assist us in this important endeavor. I will contact you during the next week regarding your response to our request.

Sincerely,

_____

Center Director

# CONSULTANT: MODIFYING CLASSROOM ENVIRONMENT

Marta Ames, M.Ed.
Anytown Educational Consultants
444 Chestnut Street
Anytown, PA 11111

Dear Ms. Ames:

We are thrilled to have engaged your services as a consultant for our program. You come highly recommended by several of our colleagues, including Alyson Watkins, Director of Alyson's Child Care Center.

As you know, our interest is in improving our classroom environments to better serve our children. As per our conversation, our staff training is scheduled for 6:00 until 8:00 PM on _____, in order to use the classrooms when children are out of the Center. We will provide staff with paper and pencils on which to draw their "dream classroom" and for recording their materials and equipment "wish lists." These materials will be forwarded to you the week before the training date.

I am enclosing a copy of our standard contract for consultant services. You may return it to me by mail, or bring it on the night of the training. We look forward to the improvements in environments that can be brought about by this training.

Sincerely,

_____

Center Director

Enc.

FIGURE 5.1

# SAMPLE CONTRACT

This contract is made between _____

                                          (agency name)

and _____ for the _____.

   (consultant/service provider name)               (description of services to be rendered)

The consultant/service provider named herein agrees to _____

_____.

     (criteria for completion of contract, timetable, dates and times of services to be provided)

For these services the consultant/service provider is to be paid the

amount of $_____, to be payable to _____,

      (agreed-upon fee/honorarium)             (how check is to be made out)

and to be paid upon _____.

                    (circumstances of payment and date due)

_____       _____

Authorized Agency Representative       Date

_____       _____

Consultant/Service Provider           Date

# CONSULTANT: INTRODUCING NEW CURRICULUM

Child Care Center

Alyson B. Watkins, M.S.W.
Director
Alyson's Child Care Center
747 Broad Street
Anytown, PA 11111

Dear Alyson:

It was so very interesting hearing about your trip to Italy and visit to Reggio Emilia! My staff and other local colleagues are intrigued and want to know more about the curriculum and the "amiable school" philosophy. Many of us have heard about Reggio Emilia, but have not had first-hand experiences with the curriculum.

I would like to invite you to attend a staff meeting at our Center on _____ at _____ to describe the highlights of your trip, review your photographs, and discuss your impressions of the curriculum. I would like to open this meeting to the local child care community.

Please contact me at _____ to advise me of your availability. I look forward to seeing you soon.

Sincerely,

_____
Center Director

# CONSULTANT: COMPUTER INSTALLATION/TRAINING

Child Care Center

Craig Murphy
Anytown Computer Consultants
222 Spruce Street
Anytown, PA 11111

Dear Mr. Murphy:

Thank you for your attentive service when I visited your business on
_____. With your assistance, I made an informed choice regarding a computer for use in our main office, and at a reasonable price. I understand that you will come to the Center on _____ at _____ to install the computer, and to provide myself and our secretary with introductory skills training.

I know that use of the upgraded computer and software will enable us to run our office more efficiently. I look forward to seeing you.

Sincerely,

_____
Center Director

© 2002 by The Center for Applied Research in Education

# CONSULTANT: DEMONSTRATION OF SOFTWARE

Craig Murphy
Anytown Computer Consultants
222 Spruce Street
Anytown, PA 11111

Dear Mr. Murphy:

We have received the material you forwarded regarding software for young children, and we are interested in several of the packages described. Please contact the Center at _____ to arrange an appointment to demonstrate the software during an upcoming staff meeting.

Many of our staff are intrigued but are unfamiliar with use of these programs with children. I believe that a demonstration of their use would allay any concerns that they have.

We look forward to hearing from you.

Sincerely,

_____
Center Director

# CONSULTANT: VISITING COLLEGE REPRESENTATIVE

Dr. Matthew Watkins
Early Childhood Education Program
Anytown Community College
605 Broad Street
Anytown, PA 11111

Dear Dr. Watkins:

Thank you for taking time to speak with me by telephone about the Early Childhood Education Program at the Anytown Community College. I am extremely interested in encouraging staff at our Center to enroll in your Associate's Degree Program. Although our lead teachers have degrees, not all have them in early childhood education. Our teacher aides and assistants tend to have inservice training experiences, but lack formal schooling in the field.

I am looking forward to your visit to our Center on _____ at _____, and to providing you with the opportunity to present an overview of the college's curriculum. Please contact me at _____ if there are any questions that I can answer prior to your visit.

Sincerely,

_____
Center Director

# CONSULTANT: DIRECTOR SEEKING CONSULTING WORK

Patricia A. Regina, Director
Anytown Child Care Center
111 Oak Street
Anytown, PA 11111

Dear Patty:

I have learned from Alyson Watkins, Director of Alyson's Child Care Center, that you are seeking a consultant to assist in the planning of your new infant room. We have had a baby room for some time at our Center. We learned a great deal in creating and implementing our plans for this space, and I would be pleased to share the process with you and your staff. I also have extensive information about infant programming and equipment.

My consulting fees are reasonable and somewhat flexible. Please contact me at our Center at _____ if you are interested in further discussing my services.

Sincerely,


_____
Center Director

# CONSULTANT: DIRECTOR'S RESPONSE TO CONSULTING REQUEST

**Child Care Center**

Patricia A. Regina, Director
Anytown Child Care Center
111 Oak Street
Anytown, PA 11111

Dear Patty:

Thank you for the opportunity to work with you and your staff on the development of your new infant-care classroom. Your community survey clearly indicates a need for this service.

As per our agreement, I will be attending your staff meetings each week for the next two months. During the first month we will be looking at the space you have selected and planning the layout of the room and equipment and materials needed. During the second month of visits, we will be setting up the classroom and working on scheduling and operational procedures (safe and healthy handling of babies, working with parents of infants, etc.).

For your convenience, I am enclosing a contract for services that outlines the details of our agreement and the fees we have discussed. Please sign and return the contract to me.

Please contact me at _____ if you have any questions or special requests. I look forward to working with you.

Sincerely,

_____

Center Director

Enc.

FIGURE 5.2

# DIRECTOR'S CONTRACT
# TO ACT AS CONSULTANT

## Child Care Center

Kathleen Pullan Watkins, Ed.D.
Durant and Watkins Associates
Educational Consultants
213 Partners Row
Anytown, PA 11111

**Contract for Consulting Services**

Kathleen Pullan Watkins, Ed.D., of the consulting firm of Durant and Watkins Associates, agrees to provide to the Director and staff of Anytown Child Care Center, 111 Oak Street, Anytown, PA 11111, a minimum of sixteen hours of consulting services for the purpose of developing and implementing an infant-care classroom at the 111 Oak Street site. The Consultant will work with the Center Director and staff during eight weekly two-hour staff meetings for a two-month period. During those meetings the Consultant will assist the client in planning room arrangement; identifying appropriate materials, equipment, and material; and scheduling and programming for infants.

The cost of these consulting services is $_____ per hour to be paid on the date of the last consultation session. The check is to be made payable to Kathleen Pullan Watkins, Ed.D.

Consultant _____ Date _____

Client _____ Date _____

# INSERVICE TRAINING: BEHAVIOR MANAGEMENT

Dr. David Goldstein
Executive Director
Anytown Child Guidance Center
217 Caterers Way
Anytown, PA 11111


Dear Dr. Goldstein:

Staff at our child care center have identified increasing numbers of children with behavior problems. Many come from homes where there are parental separations or divorces. Some children have experienced other types of family trauma, or have inconsistent caretakers in their lives.

I know the work of your Center and, while a teacher at another program, had the chance to see firsthand the positive changes you brought about working with a very troubled child. We are interested in enlisting your support via an inservice for staff training to provide information on handling child behavior problems and techniques for promoting more appropriate behavior. We are also interested in knowing the symptoms that indicate the need for specialist intervention with a child.

Please advise me at _____ of your availability. Thank you for your consideration in this matter.

Sincerely,


_____
Center Director

© 2002 by The Center for Applied Research in Education

# INSERVICE TRAINING:
# CHILD HEALTH AND SAFETY

Joan Brennan, M.D.
Medical Director
Anytown Pediatric Associates
120 Saturn Street
Anytown, PA 11111

Dear Dr. Brennan:

I have recently reviewed a copy of the *Guidelines for Child Care Center Health and Safety* that you developed for our city. I found the *Guidelines* to be clear and helpful to those of us working on the front lines with young children.

In order to better implement your ideas, I would like to invite you to visit our Center as a consultant. During your visit I would request that you observe in our classrooms and review our accident and illness policies and procedures to aid us in identifying where modifications could be made. This visit(s) would be scheduled at your convenience. Please contact me at _____ and advise me of your availability and the fee for this consultation.

I look forward to hearing from you.

Sincerely,

_____

Center Director

# INSERVICE TRAINING: MATH WORKSHOP

## Child Care Center

Gayle Jenkins
Anytown Preschool Resource Project
610 Main Street
Anytown, PA 11111

Dear Gayle:

We need your assistance to identify a trainer to conduct a math workshop for our teachers. Math and science are two weak areas in the curriculum for our program. Teachers appear to shy away from these themes because they do not feel comfortable with their own math skills. In fact, the teachers are already doing simple math and science activities with the children, but they do not realize it. I am seeking a trainer who knows how to help my teachers see that math is all around them.

Please contact me at _____ with the names of any trainer(s) who might be appropriate for our program. Thank you for your assistance in this matter.

Sincerely,

_____
Center Director

# INSERVICE TRAINING: CHILD DEVELOPMENT

Dr. Rachel Regina
Department of Psychology
Anytown Community College
605 Broad Street
Anytown, PA 11111

Dear Dr. Regina:

Through Dr. Matt Watkins of the Early Childhood Education Program at your college, I learned that you provide the child development courses for ECE students. Dr. Watkins has spoken highly of your teaching skills and rapport with students. When I mentioned my interest in bringing a trainer to our child care center to conduct workshops for our staff, he suggested that you might be interested in working with us.

We are a local child care center serving 50 children and their families. The children in our program range in age from six months to twelve years, and there are 20 caregiving, support staff and volunteers who would benefit from training. We are able to afford a reasonable honorarium for your services. If you are interested in further exploring this consulting opportunity, please contact me at _____.

Thank you for your consideration in this matter.

Sincerely,

_____
Center Director

# INSERVICE TRAINING: CHILD DEVELOPMENT ASSOCIATE TRAINING

© 2002 by The Center for Applied Research in Education

Ms. Christina Veliz
Early Childhood Education Program
Anytown Community College
605 Broad Street
Anytown, PA 11111

Dear Ms. Veliz:

I am the Director of a local child care center serving 50 children and their families. Although our lead teachers have college degrees, some are not in early childhood education. Most of our teacher aides have no training, other than that provided by the Center.

I have recently learned from Dr. Matt Watkins about the Child Development Associate Credentials. I immediately recognized this nationally known certificate as a means for staff at our Center to acquire the knowledge and skills needed for their work with young children.

Dr. Watkins informed us that you are not only a CDA trainer, but that your background includes work as a representative for the Council for Early Childhood Professional Recognition. I realize that you could not both train and assess candidates for the CDA Credential; however, I am sure that the dual experiences provide you and your trainees with unique insights.

I am interested in discussing the possibility of on-site CDA training for my staff. I have no idea of the length of time required for training or the costs involved. However, I am willing to seek outside funding for this project if necessary. If your schedule would permit you to make a commitment to conduct training and act as Advisor to six of my staff, please contact me by phone at _____.

Thank you for your consideration in this matter.

Sincerely,

_____

Center Director

# THIRD-PARTY PAYMENT FOR STAFF COLLEGE TUITION

Theresita Ramos
Cashier's Office
Anytown Community College
605 Broad Street
Anytown, PA 11111

Dear Ms. Ramos:

This letter authorizes Holly Regina, social security #555-55-5555, a staff member at our child care center, to enroll in up to four credits of Early Childhood Education Program course work at your college in the spring 2003 semester.

Our agency will cover the costs of tuition, fees, and books for Ms. Regina during the spring 2003 semester. Please contact me at _____ if further information is required.

Thank you for your assistance in this matter.

Sincerely,

_____
Center Director

# ARCHITECT: BUILDING NEW CLASSROOM SPACE

Child Care Center

Joyce M. Hampton
Hampton Architectural Associates
926 Broad Street
Anytown, PA 11111

Dear Ms. Hampton:

It was a pleasure meeting you at our Center to discuss the design for our new classroom. I was impressed with your album of past child care center projects, and I look forward to seeing your sketches for our proposed classroom. I feel that you have a good understanding of the caregiving profession and our goals for working with the children.

Please contact me as soon as the sketches are ready, and I will arrange for you to meet with the members of our Advisory Board who chair the Building Committee.

Thank you for your assistance with this project.

Sincerely,

_____

Center Director

# LANDSCAPER: REQUEST FOR BID

Child Care Center

Jason Milewski
Anytown Creative Landscaping
612 Oak Street
Anytown, PA 11111

Dear Mr. Milewski:

Thank you for visiting our Center to look over and discuss our proposed landscaping project. As you know, we are seeking a landscaper to clean up our Center property; put in a perennial flower garden and create vegetable beds that will be tended by the children; and create space for outdoor play equipment.

Our funding requires that we obtain three bids for service from any contractors. In order to consider your bid, we must receive it along with a drawing of the project in the main office no later than _____. Please provide proof of your bond and performance bond coverage. You may contact me at _____ if you require any additional information.

Sincerely,

_____

Center Director

# PLUMBER:
# UNREASONABLE ESTIMATE

Brian Purcell
Anytown Plumbing
444 Broad Street
Anytown, PA 11111

Dear Mr. Purcell:

I have received your estimate for repair of the drainage pipes in the child care center basement. I regret to inform you that your estimate is beyond what our budget permits. We have successfully secured the services of a plumber who will complete these repairs at a price that is affordable to us.

We appreciate the time you took to look at our drains and to submit an estimate to us.

Sincerely,

_____

Center Director

© 2002 by The Center for Applied Research in Education

# ELECTRICIAN: REASONABLE ESTIMATE—COMMENCE WORK

James Nicholas
Anytown Electrical Supply
921 Market Street
Anytown, PA 11111

Dear Mr. Nicholas:

Thank you for your estimate for the rewiring of the new classroom at our child care center. Your estimate was thorough and detailed, and comes within the budget for electrical work of this nature. We would like to contract with you to complete the electrical portion of this project. Please contact me at _____ to set a date for signing a contract and for the commencement of work.

Thank you for your consideration in this matter.

Sincerely,

_____
Center Director

# FOOD SERVICE: ORDER ENCLOSED

Customer Service
Anytown Food Service
444 Oak Street
Anytown, PA 11111

Dear Sir/Madam:

Enclosed is our food supply order for the month of June for our child care center. Please note the addition of canned fruit, cookies, and frozen chicken fingers to our usual order.

I can be reached at _____ during business hours if you require additional information.

Sincerely,

_____
Center Director

# FOOD SERVICE: ITEMS MISSING FROM ORDER

Elizabeth Collin
Customer Service
Anytown Food Service
444 Oak Street
Anytown, PA 11111


Dear Ms. Collin:

Thank you for talking with me by telephone regarding the items missing from our June food order. I am mystified as to how the additional items, that were especially noted in the cover letter dated _____, were excluded from our order. However, after our conversation, I have every confidence that you will immediately correct the problem. I look forward to receipt of the fruit, cookies, and frozen chicken fingers no later than _____.

You can contact me at _____ during business hours if additional information is required. Thank you for your assistance in this matter.

Sincerely,


_____
Center Director

# CHILDREN'S EQUIPMENT SUPPLIER: DEMAND FOR REFUND

**Child Care Center**

Melissa Gold
Customer Service Representative
Anytown Creative Preschool Supplies
600 Broad Street
Anytown, PA 11111

Dear Ms. Gold:

We have recently received our order #55555, placed on _____ with Anytown Creative Preschool Supplies. I was dismayed to find that all five puzzles included in item #3300 were damaged. In the past we have had excellent service from your company, and there were indicators that our orders were always carefully inspected prior to shipping. It was obvious that the puzzles were damaged prior to shipping, and I am concerned that these items were sent to us although clearly defective.

Please refund the amount of item #3300 or credit our account #1111 immediately. I have attached a copy of the invoice for this order.

Sincerely,

_____
Center Director

© 2002 by The Center for Applied Research in Education

# CHILDREN'S EQUIPMENT SUPPLIER: THANK-YOU FOR GOOD SERVICE

Melissa Gold
Customer Service Representative
Anytown Creative Preschool Supplies
600 Broad Street
Anytown, PA 11111

Dear Ms. Gold:

Thank you for your prompt attention to my letter of complaint dated _____ regarding defective materials shipped with order #55555. Not only did you credit our account for the flawed merchandise, but you also sent a set of new puzzles. As we are long-term customers of Anytown Creative Preschool Supplies, your response was appropriate and considerate. Please be assured that we will continue our patronage of your company into the future.

Thank you for your assistance in this matter.

Sincerely,

_____

Center Director

# ELECTRICIAN: DISPLEASED WITH RESULTS OF WORK

James Nicholas
Anytown Electrical Supply
921 Market Street
Anytown, PA 11111

Dear Mr. Nicholas:

I am writing to express my extreme displeasure with the electrical work completed at our child care center last month. There are exposed wires in several places that pose a hazard to children and staff. In spite of numerous telephone calls I have made to your business and messages left regarding problems with your work, you have yet to make yourself available to discuss these concerns with me.

I have called in a second contractor to examine your work, as well as an inspector from city licenses and inspections. If, as I suspect, your work is substandard, I will be contacting the Better Business Bureau.

Sincerely,


_____

Center Director

# MASON: REPAIR OF CENTER'S SIDEWALKS

Thomas W. Wilday
Anytown Masonry
200 High Street
Anytown, PA 11111

Dear Mr. Wilday:

I have received your estimate for repair of the sidewalks at our child care center. The amount that you have indicated is within our budget, and I expect you to begin work on the scheduled date next month.

As you have requested, I am enclosing a copy of the signed contract and a check in the amount of $_____, a deposit on the work to be completed. According to our agreement, you will invoice the Center $_____ for the remaining amount upon satisfactory completion of the job.

We look forward to the additionl safety that new sidewalks will provide.

Sincerely,

_____
Center Director

# VETERINARIAN: CARE OF CENTER'S PETS

## Child Care Center

Nicole Bowker, D.V.M.
Anytown Veterinary Clinic
444 Broad Street
Anytown, PA 11111

Dear Dr. Bowker:

Our family is so pleased with your care of our dog. As you know, I am director of a local child care facility. Among my many charges as administrator is the care of two parakeets, five goldfish, a rabbit, and four guinea pigs. I am concerned that these animals remain healthy, both for the sake of the animals as well as the well being of the children and staff.

I would like to retain your services to visit the Center on a once-monthly basis to care for our animals, providing immunizations or medicines as needed. It would be difficult to transport our pets to your clinic, so regular visits from you would be helpful to myself and the staff. In addition, the children would learn from your visits about the appropriate care of pets.

I will contact the Clinic to schedule your first visit and to discuss with you the fee for your visits. Thank you for your consideration in this matter.

Sincerely,

_____

Center Director

# DEPARTMENT OF PUBLIC HEALTH: CHECKS FOR LEAD PAINT

**Child Care Center**

Division of Lead Screening
Anytown Department of Public Health
117 Cherry Street
Anytown, PA 11111

Sir/Madam:

I am the director of a local child care agency providing services for 50 children and families. We are located in a converted church building that is 60 years old. Although we have had previous inspections for lead paint, I am concerned about flaking and peeling paint in the Center basement where original wall covering has been revealed. I would like to schedule an immediate visit from an inspector from your office in order to assure that none of the exposed paint is lead-based.

Our Center is open from 7:00 AM until 6:00 PM Monday through Friday. An inspector can visit us at any time during business hours.

A prompt response to my inquiry would be greatly appreciated.

Sincerely,

_____

Center Director

# CHILD CARE LICENSING

Ms. Sheila Jones
Child Care Licensing Division
State Office Building
1400 Spring Garden Street
Anytown, PA 11111


Dear Ms. Jones:

    I am writing to request forms to begin the process of relicensing our child care center. Although the five-year renewal period is a year away, I would like to receive the renewal package and review the procedures required.

    Please forward the necessary materials to me at your earliest convenience.

Sincerely,


_____

Center Director

# WORKER'S COMPENSATION INSURANCE

Countrywide Insurance Company
501 Market Street
Anytown, PA 11111

Sir/Madam:

I am the director of a local child care center with 15 employees. We currently have Worker's Compensation Insurance provided by another insurer. However, I am interested in comparing the premium we are presently paying with the rates of other companies. The state classification code for our employees is #891. Our Center has established a Safety Committee to help assure workplace safety. Please contact me regarding rates, including information about any eligibility for subclassification, the merit rating plan, and a deductible.

I can be reached at _____, if a representative wishes to call during business hours of 7:00 AM to 6:00 PM. Thank you in advance for this information.

Sincerely,

_____
Center Director

# REQUEST FOR INFORMATION ABOUT LIABILITY INSURANCE

Ms. Robin Foster, Agent
Countrywide Insurance Company
501 Market Street
Anytown, PA 11111

Dear Robin:

We have been very pleased with your prompt and efficient service regarding our Worker's Compensation Insurance. At this time I am investigating a change of insurer for our liability insurance coverage. As a child care center director I am keenly aware of the need to carry sufficient liability insurance to protect the Center against lawsuits alleging negligence.

Please forward to me information regarding your liability policies and premium rates. Thank you for your consideration in this matter.

Sincerely,

_____

Center Director

# SEND REPRESENTATIVE REGARDING PROPERTY INSURANCE

## Child Care Center

Ms. Robin Foster, Agent
Countrywide Insurance Company
501 Market Street
Anytown, PA 11111

Dear Robin:

The Advisory Board of our child care center has determined that we need to upgrade our property insurance from the basic to the special form. It is my understanding that this type of property insurance covers all forms of physical property loss unless specifically included in the policy. We also wish to add the rider for vandalism and crime insurance coverage.

Please contact me at _____ during business hours to arrange an appointment to further discuss our insurance needs. Thank you for your consideration in this matter.

Sincerely,


_____

Center Director

# POLICY FOR STAFF HEALTH INSURANCE

Ms. Robin Foster, Agent
Countrywide Insurance Company
501 Market Street
Anytown, PA 11111

Dear Robin:

Our child care center is now able to offer dental insurance for our employees. I would like to consult with you regarding the types of policies that are available through your office. I am specifically interested in acquiring Northfield Dental coverage, as I feel that their policy is liberal and inclusive. Please provide me with a comparison of the coverage offered by several companies. If your company cannot provide coverage directly, perhaps you can refer me to the appropriate insurer.

Thank you for ongoing quality service and, in advance, for the information regarding dental insurance.

Sincerely,

_____

Center Director

# PROBLEMS WITH STAFF HEALTH-INSURANCE CLAIM

Child Care Center

Yvette Monroe
Customer Service Supervisor
Claims Department
Northfield Dental
126 Partners Row
Anytown, PA 11111

Dear Ms. Monroe:

As per our conversation on _____, I am writing regarding a claim made by one of our staff against policy #9999. Ms. Deborah Johnson, a teacher at our child care center, is covered under this policy provided to all employees. I am concerned because according to my own copy of the policy, identical to that of all other Center staff, tooth capping is a permissible claim at a 100% reimbursement rate.

Although Ms. Johnson has talked with several representatives of your company, she has been unable to get a satisfactory response regarding denial of her claim. Please review this claim and contact Ms. Johnson at your earliest convenience with a detailed response to her claim.

Thank you for your cooperation in this matter.

Sincerely,

_____
Center Director

# BIBLIOGRAPHY

Bellm, D., et al. *The Early Childhood Mentoring Curriculum: A Handbook for Mentors.* National Center for the Early Childhood Work Force, 1997.

Billamn, J. *Starting and Operating a Child Care Center.* Brown and Benchmark, 1993.

Bloom, P.J. *Blueprint for Action: Achieving Center-Based Change through Staff Development.*

Bredekamp, S. and C. Copple. (Eds.). *Developmentally Appropriate Practice in Early Childhood Programs.* National Association for the Education of Young Children, 1997.

Chehrazi, S.S. *Psychosocial Issues in Day Care.* American Psychiatric Press, Inc., 1997.

Cherry, C. *Family Day Care Providers Management Guide.* Fearon Teachers Aids, 1996.

Clarke, J.I. *Who, Me Lead a Group?* Parenting Press, Inc., 1998.

Click, P.M. and D.W. Click. *Administration of Schools for Young Children.* Delmar, 1996.

Copeland, T. *The Business Guide to Family Child Care Record Keeping.* Redleaf Press, 1997.

Copeland, T. *Family Child Care Inventory-Keeper: The Complete Log for Depreciating and Insuring Your Property.* Redleaf Press, 1999.

Copeland, T. *Marketing Guide: How to Build Enrollment and Promote Your Business as a Child Care Professional.* Redleaf Press, 1999.

Crosiar, S.J., et al. *Training School-Age Child Care Staff: A Handbook for Workshop Leaders.* Cornell University Cooperative Extension, 1995.

Daley, S.P. and K.A. Guy. *Welcome the Child: A Child Advocacy Guide for Churches.* Friendship Press, 1994.

Decker, C.A. and J.R. Decker. *Planning and Administering Early Childhood Programs.* Prentice Hall, 1995.

Donowitz, L.G. (Ed.). *Infection Control in the Child Care Center and Preschool,* 4th Edition. Wilma E. Rosenberg, 1999.

Edelstein, S. *Nutrition and Meal Planning in Child Care Programs: A Practical Guide.* American Dietetics Association, 1992.

Evans, F.J. *Managing the Media: Proactive Strategies for Better Business-Press Relations.* Greenwood Publishing Group, Inc., 1987.

Feeney, S. and N.K. Freeman. *Ethics and the Early Childhood Educator: Using the NAEYC Code*. National Association for the Education of Young Children, 1999.

Ferry, T.S. *Child Care Safety*. American Society of Safety Engineers, 1993.

Frank, M. (Ed.). *Child Care: Emerging Legal Issues*. Haworth Press, 1983.

Gallagher, P.C. *Start Your Own At-Home Child Care Business*, 2nd Edition. The Young Sparrow Press, 1995.

Garner, B.P. *Room to Grow: The Physical Environment for Infants and Toddlers*. Southern Early Childhood Association.

Godwin, A. and L. Schrag (Eds.). *Settings for Infant/Toddler Care: Guidelines for Centers and Family Child Care Homes*. National Association for the Education of Young Children, 1996.

Gofflin, S.G. and J. Lombardi. *Speaking Out: Early Childhood Advocacy*. National Association for the Education of Young Children, 1988.

Greenman, J. *Caring Spaces, Learning Places: Children's Environments That Work*. Child Care Information Exchange, 1988.

Hanlon, T.W. *Y.M.C.A. Preschool Age Child Care*. Human Kinetics Press, 1995.

Harms, T. *Infant/Toddler Environment Rating Scale*. Teachers College Press, 1990.

Harms, T. *School-Age Care Environment Rating Scale*. Teachers College Press, 1995.

Hawkins, N.I. and H.K. Rosenholtz. *Profitable Child Care: How to Start and Run a Successful Business*. Facts on File, 1993.

Hildebrand, V. and P.F. Hearron. *Management of Child Development Centers*. Macmillan Publishing, 1996.

Jennings, G. *Successful Day Nursery Management*. LPC/InBook, 1994.

Jensen, M.A. *Issues and Advocacy in Early Childhood Education*. Allyn and Bacon, Inc., 1999.

Kagan, S.L. and B.T. Bowman (Eds.). *Leadership in Early Care and Education*. National Association for the Education of Young Children, 1997.

Kalin, J. *Home Day Care Handbook: A Caregiver's Guide to Operating a Home Day Care Business*, 1999.

King, M.A., et al. *Creating a Child-Centered Day Care Environment for Two-Year-Olds*. Charles C. Thomas Publisher, 1993.

Lewis, J.G. and L.D. Renn. *How to Start and Manage a Day Care Center Business: Step by Step Guide to Business Success*. Lewis and Renn Associates, 1999.

Lewis, J.G. and L.D. Renn. *How to Start and Manage a Child Care Services Business: A Practical Way to Start Your Own Business*. Lewis and Renn Associates, 1999.

McGregor-Loundes, et al. (Eds.). *Legal Issues for Non-Profit Associations*. Cavendish Publishing, 1996.

Moore, G.T. *Early Childhood Physical Environment Observation Schedule and Rating Scales: Preliminary Scales for the Measurement of the Physical Environment of Child Care Centers and Related Environments*. University of Wisconsin-Milwaukee, 1995.

NAEYC. *Congregations and Child Care: A Self-Study for Churches and Synagogues and Their Early Childhood Programs*. National Association for the Education of Young Children, 1990.

NAEYC. *NAEYC Accreditation Criteria and Procedures: Position Statement of the National Academy of Early Childhood Programs*. National Association for the Education of Young Children, 1984.

Nelson, M.K. *Negotiated Care: The Experience of Family Day Care Providers*. Temple University Press, 1990.

Neugebauer, B. *The Anti-Ordinary Thinkbook: A Stimulating Tool for Staff Training and Team Building*. Child Care Information Exchange, 1991.

Neugebauer, R. *Developing Staff Skills*. Child Care Information Exchange, 1990.

Neugebauer, R. *Fostering Improved Staff Performance*. Child Care Information Exchange, 1991.

Neugebauer, R. *Inside Child Care: Trend Report*. Child Care Information Exchange, 1997.

Neugebauer, R. *250 Management Success Stories: From Child Care Center Directors*. Child Care Information Exchange, 1995.

Neugebauer, R. *On Being a Leader*. Child Care Information Exchange, 1990.

Neugebauer, R. *On-Target Marketing. Promotion Strategies for Child Care Centers*. Child Care Information Exchange, 1996.

Neugebauer, R. *Parent Relations: Building an Active Partnership*. Child Care Information Exchange, 1994.

Neugebauer, R. *Survival Skills for Center Directors*. Child Care Information Exchange, 1996.

Neugebauer, R. *Taking Stock: Tools for Teacher, Director, and Center Evaluation*. Child Care Information Exchange, 1994.

Neugebauer, R. and B. Neugebauer. *The Art of Leadership: Managing Early Childhood Organizations*. Child Care Information Exchange, 1998.

Neugebauer, R. and B. Neugebauer. *Does Your Team Work? Ideas for Bringing Your Staff Together*. Child Care Information Exchange, 1997.

Neugebauer, R. and B. Neugebauer. *Managing Money: A Center Director's Guidebook*. Child Care Information Exchange, 1997.

Neugebauer, R. and B. Neugebauer. *Top 20 Classics: The Best of Exchange from the First 20 Years*. Child Care Information Exchange, 1998.

Prentice-Hall (Eds.). *Start Your Own Childcare Business*. Prentice Hall, 1995.

Pressma, D. and L.J. Emery. *Serving Children: HIV Infection in Children in Day Care*. Child Welfare League of America, 1991.

Pruissen, C.M. *Start and Run a Profitable Home Day Care*. Self-Counsel Press, 1998.

Rab, V.Y., et al. *Child Care and the ADA: A Handbook for Inclusive Programs*. Paul H. Brookes, 1997.

Richard, M.M. *Before and After School Programs: A Start-up and Administration Manual*. School-Age Notes, 1991.

Robinson, L.M. *Hire and Keep Child Care Staff*. Readers Press, 1997.

Robinson, L.M. *Start and Operate a Child Care Center*. Readers Press, 1997.

Rodd, J. *Leadership in Early Childhood: The Pathway to Professionalism*. Teachers College Press, 1999.

Schiller, P.B. and P.M. Dyke. *Managing Quality Child Care Centers: A Comprehensive Manual for Administrators*. Teachers College Press, 1995.

Sciarra, D.J. and A.G. Dorsey. *Developing and Administering a Child Care Center*. Delmar, 1998.

Shoemaker, C. *Administration and Management of Programs for Young Children*. Prentice Hall, 1995.

Shoemaker, C. *Leadership and Management of Programs for Young Children*. Prentice Hall, 1999.

Simmons, T. *How to Own and Operate Your Own Home Day Care Business without Going Nuts!: The Day Care Survival Handbook and Guide for Aspiring Home Day Care Providers*. Amber Books, 1999.

Steelsmith, S. *How to Start a Home-Based Day-Care Business*. Globe Pequot Press, 1997.

Taylor, B.J. *Early Childhood Program Management: People and Procedures*. Prentice Hall, 1996.

Watkins, K.P. and L. Durant. *The Complete Book of Forms for Managing the Preschool Program*. Center for Applied Research in Education, 1990.

Weinstein, C.S. *Spaces for Dollars: The Built Environment and Child Development*. Perseus Books, 1987.

Westman, J.C. *Who Speaks for the Children?: The Handbook of Individual and Class Child Advocacy*. Professional Resource Exchange, 1991.

Wipfler, P. *Leading a Parent Resource Group*. Parents Leadership Institute, 1990.